UNDIAGNOSED

The Ugly Side of

Dyslexia

By Ameer Baraka

McCoral Publishing

Dedication

To my grandma, who passed away without being aware of my dyslexia

I'm eternally thankful you taught me how to love family, people, and life. Your inability to teach me to read was not your fault. I wish you had the opportunity to hear me testify before the United States Senate. You only got to see one of the films I was in. When I walked the red carpet with your daughter, my beloved mom, by my side, we both felt your presence.

I made something of myself, grandma. I know you are pleased, but I still haven't done enough. I need to help more kids like me. All I want is for you to smile. I wish you could see me now. I'm visiting schools and prisons, telling people about education and God's love.

Thank you, and I'm so sorry my actions in my early life made you cry.

CONTENTS

CONTENTS

FOREWORD

I sat in the airport and read Ameer's story. While I sat there reading something that I knew had only been in the hands of so few individuals, I would glance up at the constant stream of people and wonder who was living a life of heartache and limited potential, just like Ameer, because of a challenge with reading. I wondered who was keeping the secret. I felt like I was sitting there with the secret of Ameer's story and my secret of what to do as an educator. I wanted to stand on my worn-out airport chair, shake my fists in the air, and tell everyone that we collectively failed Ameer, and I didn't want to see that happen to anyone else.

Ameer's story felt eerily familiar to me because I could have easily been one of his teachers. I could have been the teacher that didn't know how to identify his dyslexia or realize that his behavior was the symptom of something else. I could have been the one that passed him to the next grade because I definitely didn't want him in my class the following year. This felt so familiar because, as a young educator, I would put tracing papers in front of my students, and as their tiny hands traced the letter "A," I felt like I was teaching them how to read. We would read books daily in a reading circle and talk about them, and I felt like I was preparing them to be readers. That reading circle was beautiful; however, I didn't know what I didn't know. Likewise, Ameer's teachers didn't know what they didn't know. There is a principle in reading instruction called the Peter Effect, taken from the Apostle Peter in Acts 3:5, who, when asked for money by a beggar, stated that he could not give what he did not have. The Peter Effect states that you cannot be expected to give what you do not possess. In other words, you cannot teach what you do not know. Research tells us that educators are not being prepared in their pre-service programs to teach reading. They don't know, so how could a teacher recognize Ameer's lack of reading development and, more importantly, how could they have intervened with the appropriate evidence-based instruction that is essential for learning to read for the largest portion of the population. Only a small percentage of students learn to read effortlessly; the other students need a systematic approach. If I had been Ameer's teacher when I was in the classroom, I would have failed him.

However, shame and blame should not sit squarely on the shoulders of teachers. Our pre-service programs have not been preparing educators with the knowledge needed to teach reading according to what is true and evident from scientific research. An EdWeek report from 2019 states that only 11% of educators feel entirely confident in teaching reading due to their pre-service programs and training. This means that 89% of educators were like me when I started teaching, and 89% are like Ameer's teachers. As a result, hundreds of thousands of students are at risk of living through incomprehensible circumstances because we've failed to prepare educators.

I've been in education for over 25 years, first as a teacher, then as an administrator, and now leading thousands of educators nationally in communities and through professional learning on the Science of Reading. The journey to where I am today took dedicated learning, intentional time, and a never-ending curiosity to discover what I didn't know. I didn't start this learning journey until after I left the classroom, and that is one of my biggest regrets and sources of guilt. I wonder how many students like Ameer passed through my doors, and I never knew what to do. While in the classroom, I had a prime opportunity and didn't jump at the chance to learn because I never understood the urgency of Literacy. Once my curiosity and deep desire to learn kicked in, I got certified as an Academic Language Practitioner and got my Ph.D. in Literacy and Educational Leadership. Now that I know better about how we learn to read, I lead on a national level to ensure that no teacher has to run into the classroom being as ill-equipped as I was. I have such an empathetic heart for Ameer's teachers. I want to speak understanding, life, and hope to every teacher to ensure that students do not have to endure the misery that Ameer faced in the classroom and fueled the version of himself that led to destruction.

Ameer's story is an undeniable example of why there is such an urgency in Literacy. What captured my mind the most was how he saw the world as a young child. Because he couldn't read, he couldn't see a world outside his own. He couldn't see examples and mentors that could show him what contributing to a community could look like. Ameer quotes Marian Wright Edelman, Founder and President of the Children's Defense Fund, who said, "You can't be what you can't see." Ameer didn't have access to words, stories, adventures, and examples of Black men who led their families through honest work. He couldn't see beyond his current circumstances, and this lack of skill in reading manifested as stress, anxiety, impulsive behavior, feelings of worthlessness, and worse, a mindset that said look out for yourself and don't let anyone, even Tim, a fellow drug dealer, stand in your way.

As a practitioner in an evidence-based approach to reading, I get calls every spring from crying mommas telling me they got my name and number, usually from someone I don't know myself, and they need help. They tell me stories through pain and despair, how their child sobs on the way to school, how they have become discouraged, and just plain sad. I can't say no to these crying mommas. Oh, how I wish I could have gotten a call from Ameer's mom. Oh, how I wish I could have been a part of his story in this new version of myself that knows what to do. That's why this book is so fundamental for me. This book declares, no, this book demands for our society to understand the epic need to turn our collective attention to the urgency in Literacy. With every passing day, another student sinks, another student cries themselves to sleep, and another life will not live to see the next day because of suicide. Literacy defines class status; it is a driver in the high stakes of poverty and determines the quality of life. But that's not all; being able to read impacts our skilled workforce; if you can't read well, your employment options are limited. In addition, there are intricate and woven threads of reading in everyday life, such as shopping for groceries, healthcare for yourself and your family, and ordering off the menu at a restaurant. I have had the distinct honor and privilege to learn at the feet of hundreds of parents and students that struggle with reading. Their educational journey has shaped their place in society. I can see the pain, feel the heartache, and know their trek through school and life has been kept secret and hidden from a world that needs to be invested and educated about what we can do correctly and do better.

This book is now my battle cry! Every educator, administrator, and member of society needs to adopt this book as their battle cry to work tirelessly for students. We must constantly assess students and resource our educators, parents, and stakeholders. It should be a never-ending cycle. In addition, every student needs to adopt this book as their anthem and find comfort in the pages of knowing they are not alone. Their actions may not mirror Ameer's, but their pain and heartache do. Finally, every student needs to see Ameer as a role model of how to claw their way into an unknown and scary world of self-acceptance and prosperity and into a place where words can walk through their minds and hearts that lead to a fruitful and fulfilled life.

As a leader in the education space, this book helps me to cast a vision for what needs to happen in our society to be the spark in lighting a passion and fire in the urgency of Literacy:

- College preparation programs must be held accountable for providing pre-service programs that align with the Science of Reading and equip educators to run headlong into classrooms being fully prepared and resourced.
- Educators need in-service coaches and communities to stay on top of the research, learn, and grow together in a non-judgmental, safe and authentic environment.
- The banquet table should be set, and all stakeholders should be invited to address the Literacy crisis: students, parents, educators, administrators, community members, business owners, healthcare professionals, criminal justice professionals for youth and adults, and any other stakeholder that I have failed to mention.
- Students must be screened early. I'll repeat it for those in the back that didn't hear. Students must, and without question, be screened early.
- Students who do not learn to read effortlessly must be taught to read with an evidence-based approach.
- We should ALL see ourselves as Literacy Leaders to drive positive outcomes, realizing that leadership is about your values, traits, and characteristics.

- Educators and administrators need a mindset that leads toward change, growth, and learning in Literacy.
- Parents should be involved in the education process and taught about reading instruction.

While Ameer's story is revealing, raw, honest, and often made me sit in disbelief and squirm in my airport chair, the pure joy of triumph can be felt. I was rooting for Ameer while he was in prison. I was rooting for the individuals that finally diagnosed him with dyslexia. I found myself smiling in that airport when I came to the book's close and realized that if Ameer could rise from the unspeakable story through God's glory and grace, and with targeted instruction in reading, there is hope. I will carry that torch of hope with this book, alongside Ameer, to reach thousands of educators and students.

Dr. Terrie Noland
V.P. of Educator Initiatives for Learning Ally

INTRODUCTION

I am compelled to write about how learning to read saved my life. How I broke free of the school to prison pipeline. How one diagnosis of an invisible disability called dyslexia became a doorway out of prison and a pathway that led to Hollywood's doorstep. I am obligated to every young child and grown adult who cannot read (yet) to share my life story in hopes that a different tomorrow is possible. If I can read, I can dream.

I want to tell you about redemption and the small acts of mentorship that change dark to beautiful. My story is both ugly and hopeful, real and all too common. A life that ultimately led to triumph began in the dog eat dog streets of New Orleans. If the foundation builds the house, my foundation had all the signs of a condemned home waiting to fall in on itself. The walls slowly closed in, and predictably, the floor fell out from under my feet. I felt I had no other place to call home but the volatile streets. The dark side may be easier, but the consequences can be lethal.

I am here to prove that rehabilitation is not only possible but essential in addressing learning difficulties. Before another child suffers the same fate, I want to shout from all the rooftops that academic performance and early screening for learning differences are essential to keeping children safe so they grow up exploring their full potential and being supported into who they can become. When children are backed into an educational corner, children underestimate themselves until crime seems like their only option. Drugs, poverty, or death claim them. To escape violence as a society and in our communities, we must attend to our most vulnerable citizens: our children. If they can't read, they can't believe they have a choice. Let's ensure they do more than just survive; let's ensure they thrive.

I hope to make a difference in others' lives by showing through determination and education that there is an alternative to incarcerated youth and a method to guarantee the school to prison pipeline is dismantled once and for all.

Dyslexia mentally incarcerated me before I ever got to a juvenile detention center. After learning to read as a young man in my twenties, I freed myself from the streets and found my self-worth. The road was long and painful to get here. I want every child from the projects and all corners of this great country to find the freedom to realize their fullest potential. May the attention around dyslexia grow and grow until no child suffers in silence and every child is granted the human right to read.

On May 10, 2016, Senator Cassidy chaired Health, Education and Labor and Pensions (HELP) Committee hearing on understanding dyslexia, and I testified before the United States Senate. I shared my life experiences with the intention of shining a spotlight on how prevalent dyslexia is among those incarcerated in the prison system and how reading difficulties shaped me as a person, leading me and so many fellow inmates down a path of violence and self-destruction. In December 2018, Senator Cassidy's provision providing for the screening of inmates for dyslexia was included in the new version of the First Step Act.

Even though we got one step further through this legislation, there is still a long way ahead. We need to catch dyslexia before kids turn to a life of crime. Our country's youth cannot afford to wait for diagnosis until they are behind bars. The right time or place for diagnosis is not after incarceration within the prison system but during early childhood education within the school system.

I am not proud of what I did in my youth, but I am grateful for the person I've become. My intention is to help spread awareness about how an undiagnosed learning difference causes ripple effects; how education failure can turn into a tidal wave of potential violence and devastation. I can never give back the life I stole that night in the streets, but I can help people understand why and how I came to be in a position to commit the crimes I did. I can explain to those who are where I was that there are other paths to take that lead to much better places in life.

INTRODUCTION

Here is my testimony:

"Good morning, Senators. I want to thank you for taking your valuable time to listen to my message. We are coming upon an important Presidential election, and I know your time is important. I'm also not oblivious to the challenges we face as a country. One such challenge is the life-long curse of dyslexia. One out of five lives with this challenge each day of their lives. So, many will never reach their full potential and enjoy this great country as you and I do. So many people have lost the will to believe because the enemy, dyslexia, has forced them into the shadows. But today, we have found a new way to address this enemy once and for all.

For many years I allowed dyslexia to control my life and rob me of my God-given potential. Can you imagine in my early teens never wanting to be anything but a drug dealer? Neither my mother nor my school teachers were able to diagnose the reasons why I had trouble learning. In my mind, pursuing a more formal education was irrelevant. I knew early in life that being a dentist, physical therapist, or lawyer was out of my reach because I could NOT read. I turned to quicker pathways out of the New Orleans projects. I saw men in my community making ways for themselves without having to read by selling drugs. And my defeatist attitude seemed to outweigh the positive values my grandmother tried to teach me. There were many more ingredients that helped me make my decision to sell drugs. For example, having my mother and siblings call me names such as "dumb and stupid." Using names such as these can cause any child to feel hopeless and lost.

If you notice, I never mentioned my father in this presentation. That's because he left when I was three years old to chase his dreams of finding a better grade of heroin to use. It was the perfect storm for me. I chose to succumb to my environment while both my brother and sister excelled in school. I didn't care about my future or anyone else because I thought I was a dummy like my mother and siblings said.

I became a street thug and full of anger because I felt cheated out of an education. I went to school just because I had to as a kid. Many

Fridays, I would "malinger" because I couldn't pass the spelling test. Or I would sleep in project hallways until school was out to avoid embarrassment. I pushed myself into a hole, and I couldn't get out of it. My teachers had to know that I couldn't read. My young mother ran the streets and didn't seem to value my education. But what became the final thing that caused me to pledge my allegiance to the lies of the streets was a girl. I was in sixth grade, and the girl I liked was in class. It was our first week of school. We were in English class, and the teacher called upon me to read out loud. My palms began to sweat, and it felt like drops of blood on my forehead. I couldn't pronounce any of the words, and the teacher made me continue, knowing that I couldn't read. Some students laughed while others looked in amazement. From that day forward, I knew that school wasn't the place for me. And the young lady never really liked me much from that day forward. The streets became my classroom and looking back, the lessons I learned were shameful. I shot and killed a young person because the streets taught me that is how you resolve conflict. After my release from prison at fifteen years of age for manslaughter, I got back into the drug game, still never learning to read, I ended up doing prison time as an adult.

I ran from the law for four years as a fugitive because I was facing sixty years for drug distribution, and I was guilty. I ended up doing four years by God's grace; a jury found me guilty of a lesser charge. At age twenty-three, I entered a prison correctional facility reading at a third-grade level. I didn't feel bad because many of the men there were just like me. We all read poorly. But after reading the Autobiography of Malcolm X, I discovered that he dropped out in seventh grade and still made something of himself. I thought for the first time in my life that I could accomplish something too. I worked hard, writing down each word I couldn't pronounce. I just kept memorizing words and writing letters, and reading short books.

A GED teacher noticed that I was struggling with phonics and had me tested. He asked if my siblings could read. I told him that my siblings went to college. After testing me, he said that I had a reading disability, and it could be corrected if I was willing to work hard.

I would write words down wrong, so I sat in front of the class to double-check. I worked for four years trying to attain my GED. My reading ability had surged, and I was ready to take the test. I passed and started helping others in math and vocabulary building. Since my release from prison, I went on to model for clothing lines like Nike. Also, I went to acting class and worked with the Academy Award winner Jessica Lange, Kathy Bates, Angela Bassett, Forest Whitaker, Blair Underwood, Hill Harper, and many others. I produced four independent films and wrote my first book, The Life I Chose: The Streets Lied to Me. It is meant to inspire others who are just like I was, hiding in the shadows and not getting help. It is also for those who believe that dealing drugs is not the way out. Today, there are schools available for kids to fight dyslexia, schools such as the Cassidys.

Thank you for your time and consideration."

Chapter 1

THE BEGINNINGS

On November 29, at 11 p.m., I was born into this world at a whopping ten pounds. A weight not nearly as heavy as my young mother must have carried as she gave birth all alone, without her husband beside her. She was still a teenager when she had me, her third baby.

My dad, Otis, proudly gave me the name Ameer Baraka Harris, although he was nowhere near the hospital when I was born. I imagine my dad was as high as a kite at the time of my arrival, a million miles away from the hard reality that there was now an additional mouth to feed.

My father was a strikingly good-looking, well-educated street junkie, so I was told. I never really knew much about my dad. He was more 'absentee' than 'father.' He disappeared from my life when I was three, and I didn't meet him again until I was eighteen.

Almost all I knew about my father came from overhearing grown-ups' comments and conversations about him. I gathered he was always fast-talking, carried a newspaper under his arm everywhere he went, and had a distinct passion for talking people on the streets of New Orleans right out of their money.

No one seemed to understand why my dad used drugs. He did not grow up in poverty. His family was educated and scholarly. I learned that his only sister died in a car crash. On a winding country road, she lost control and crashed her car, making him an instant only child. Maybe the accident contributed to his habit. The loss could've been the cause that first led him to use. After the accident, he was his parents' center of attention and was doted upon by his entire family. Somewhere along the way, he got the message that he could get away with whatever he wanted. He'd always wanted to be an engineer. My mother longed for him to take that road, but he never chose to pursue his dream.

My mother, on the other hand, was a semi-constant. My mother's skin was as black as an inner-city project's hallway. She stood at a stately five foot ten inches tall with full lips. People often said she was 'fine,' like new money. All she really wanted was a family and to please her husband, who was always 'in and out' of our lives. They would divorce in 1986.

She went to college for two years before dropping out. She didn't want to earn a living by doing physical labor like my grandmother and decided to learn to type instead. She worked for the city of New Orleans at The Sewage and Water Board for almost twenty-five years. She was a supervisor and a single mom who took pride in her position and made sure to keep her job to ensure our economic standing. Her workplace may have had a stench, but it was a stable job, and they valued her work.

My friends' mothers did not have jobs. Growing up, my mother was one of the only women I knew (except one other mom down the street) who woke up every morning and went to work. She made decent money; we always had a place to live, clean clothes on our backs, and food on the table.

My mother tried her best to shield her children from the reality of the projects, but nonetheless, hard lessons slipped through the cracks. While my mother portrayed a happy front to us, she suffered intensely and silently. I don't remember much about my dad from my early childhood. However, the one unfortunate memory I do recall is my dad's violence towards my mother. At age three, one of my first memories was hearing excruciating screams coming from the kitchen. I tentatively crept towards the dreadful sounds and peeked around the corner. My young eyes registered that my father had hurt my mother. I saw him pull her hair, and he repeatedly struck her in the head as she tried to cover her face.

Although I only remember that one incident, I know many more occurred. That is all I remember of my dad. No small hugs, no father and son conversations, no family trips. Nothing but domestic violence and the unprocessed trauma that drove him to raise his fists at the mother of his children.

My siblings and I lived in the third ward of the Calliope Project, also known as the B. W. Cooper Public Housing Development, located in the city of New Orleans. The third ward was one of the most dangerous sections of the development, where the hard-headed killers and the biggest drug dealers lived.

The Calliope Project was especially notorious for its extremely high violent crime rate. Throughout the eighties and nineties, my home neighborhood had the infamous distinction as one of the most violent housing projects in the entire country. It was a low-slung development with five porches to a building, each with four different units. Urine, piles of broken glass, discarded drug needles, and constant gunshots punctuated small talk.

Despite all this, project life was fun for us kids. Those porches were all we knew, and we made our world enjoyable. Human beings, especially children in high-stress environments, are nothing but adaptable. However, the internalized consequences of that level of constant threat detection in my developing brain cannot be understated. It was an extremely dangerous place to live, and we all knew it.

At Calliope, everybody knew everybody's business. This was one of the primary social downfalls of living in the projects. Despite knowing the reality of what kids were up to, everyone practiced a "know nothing, see nothing, hear nothing, do nothing" attitude. This was the ghetto motto and an unspoken creed we all lived by. Even when people knew something was wrong, they just looked the other way and pretended not to notice. Sometimes, a collective survival instinct looks like no one really cares at all.

My maternal grandmother lived in the projects, too, and played a huge part in raising me. She came from the cotton fields of Mississippi and was a hard worker. She cleaned houses and washed clothes for affluent white people who mostly worked in the New Orleans' Garden District.

She was a tough lady who didn't let anyone even think about walking over her (or us, for that matter). When I was younger, I felt good about my grandmother's protection. One day I got into a fight, and she came outside to defend me by *actually* jumping on top of the older boy I was fighting with. When his mother came out and got involved in the confrontation, my grandmother ran inside and came back out with a knife. "I dare you to come back down here," she taunted.

My mother had one brother, Robert, from a different father. I never met my maternal grandfather, which was quite common in the projects. But my Uncle Robert's dad, Oscar, had a big white Cadillac, and everyone took notice when he came around. I didn't know him well and often wondered where he lived, how he got that fancy car, or why we never visited him at his house. To him, we were ghetto children. I guess he didn't want to be associated too closely or play an integral part in our world.

My grandmother still loved her ex-husband, Oscar, very much, and I believe that is the reason she treated her new boyfriend, Walter, so poorly. Walter was an uneducated, alcoholic countryman and a jack of all trades. He took care of us like we were his own grandchildren. I never met my mother's father, but for a long time, I wished Walter was my grandfather.

Walter and Oscar never got along because they both loved my grandmother. Even though Walter wasn't always around, when he showed up, he was affectionate. He bought us cookies and candy. I knew that I was his favorite grandkid. I stayed up late with him and my grandmother. They drank beer and talked about how good country living would be. They dreamt of moving out of the projects and having a house and a piece of land far from the city one day.

Every Friday, Walter brought the family downtown to visit my grandmother's sister. I truly cared for my great aunt's husband, Charlie. Charlie was a white man. Walter and Uncle Charlie would tell us stories about a ghost who lived in the old abandoned house across the street. The story seemed so real that I often thought I saw that ghost in our own home. I was terrified. Uncle Charlie sat in his big, white rocking chair and smoked cigars. Since I had a white uncle, my attention to skin color was different than some of my peers. My white uncle and lighter-skinned cousins were all part of my family, so they were just relatives to me. This fact contributed to my lack of hate toward white people–unlike many of my friends in the projects who developed deep racial distrust and prejudice. I often had arguments with my friends when my relatives visited. My friends and neighbors teased me incessantly for having white people in my family.

When I was nine years old, I found out that my great aunt didn't like my mother because she was dark-skinned. My great aunt had married a white man, and all her kids had fair complexions. Her family saw my mom as an outcast and mistreated her. I saw how this affected my mother. She rarely wanted to spend time with her family; they blatantly made her shy and withdrawn. They never had high hopes for us 'darker-skinned' children from the projects.

I had two older siblings growing up: my sister, Russhan, is three years older and my older brother, Dash, short for Dashan, is a year older. My family never called me Ameer; they called me by my nickname, Milly.

My family wasn't as hard on me as they were on my other siblings, I guess in part because I was the baby. I was spoiled with sweets and consequently developed a rotten tooth (since no one ever told me to brush my teeth). I was so mad when I lost my permanent tooth. I was only a child, and I felt someone should have instructed me to brush my teeth or at least reminded me to do so.

My mother always took me to her house and left Dash and Russhan to stay with my grandmother. Even though our homelife was often filled with activity and friends, there were definitely gaps in our care. My grandmother filled in those gaps as best as she could, but looking back, I see how much we needed both parents to parent us.

Chapter 2

UNDIAGNOSED

My grandmother made sure education was first in our lives. I'd watch my grandmother put the spelling words on an old chalkboard. Russhan and Dash would be in deep trouble if they didn't know their words. I recall one night, Dash couldn't spell his words correctly. My grandmother made him put his hands out in front of him and hit him with a belt until his hands were swollen and red.

Dash was a good kid and at least three times brighter than I thought I'd ever be. Somehow, I was off the hook to participate in the required spelling word lists, perhaps because my grandmother saw how much I struggled, or again because I was the youngest. I watched my older siblings rise week after week to their spelling challenges. My grandmother spared me the spanking when I was younger–that was–until I entered third grade. She thought something was a little 'off' with me since I struggled so much with reading and writing. The mystery of why I was different from my siblings in spelling and writing development wouldn't be revealed until much, much later. Though I didn't have to feel the pain of corporal punishment at first, the hurt was still pretty deep in the long run. She couldn't have known then that no amount of spanking could have willed me, a dyslexic child, to read and write. If they'd only known.

Unlike me, Russhan and Dash loved school. In comparison, I did so poorly academically that I felt like an outsider in my own family. All my effort was invisible to everyone else but me, with absolutely no measurable result or reward. Studies and MRI brain imaging have noted that dyslexic students use four times as much energy to read as non-dyslexic students. I had no interest in school because it was so hard for me to focus, and I lacked even the most basic reading skills. I failed to learn simple phonics, so everything else, every other subject, seemed foreign and unmanageable. Reading was everywhere, and I couldn't do it. It was as if the teachers were speaking another language to me. All. Day. Long.

By third grade (by all accounts, the most important year for measuring future academic success), teachers began noticing I had fallen way behind. I simply had no idea what I was doing in the classroom, and neither did anyone else. Feeling lost, that sinking feeling of seeing everyone move ahead while not even pretending to keep up–that was me.

Cheating was the only way I knew how to pass a test. I can recall one incident in third grade where I had written the words for a spelling test down on my hand. The teacher caught me and spanked me in the bathroom. Again, the message was clear. Violence was a consequence for not measuring up. I knew cheating was wrong, but it was the only way I had even the remotest chance to pass a test, *especially* spelling. I just couldn't catch on, and not one adult, not one teacher thought to dig a little further to see if there was something causing me to struggle. In the end, I had to repeat third grade.

At that tender age of seven to nine years old, the developing sense of self is crucial for a child's identity and social-emotional well-being. A third-grader begins to see themselves in relationship to others and knows if they belong. Who was I? I was the kid who watched all my peers advance while I was held back. I was the kid who didn't compare to my siblings. I was the kid who cheated and couldn't rise to the intellectual feats other students seemed to grasp with ease. I could NOT read. What did that say about me? What was wrong with me, and where did I belong? What could I ever become in life?

For a very long time, I hated my mother and grandmother for not taking my education more seriously. I saw how much they pushed Dash and Russhan, and I felt neglected, like I was the forgotten child–unimportant and not worth as much of their time and energy. They tried to instill a sense of my siblings' drive and desire for education. Instead, I felt left behind, alone, in the dark, lost in a sea of confusing words that never made sense.

All that talk about me being the baby didn't massage my anger, and by the middle of third grade, I began avoiding school altogether. Not being able to read hindered my interest and was simply too embarrassing to face.

By the time my grandmother tried the chalkboard during my third-grade year and beat my hands with the belt, it was much too late. I was so far behind, and I already hated school with a passion. I needed a specialized, explicit, sensory-based education style. A traditional or non-phonics-based approach would not register with my brain. My grandmother didn't know that. No one did.

I decided not to go to school one day and took a nice nap in the project hallway. A family friend brought me inside his apartment and questioned me for what seemed like hours. He never disclosed to my family that I was skipping school. Whether right or wrong, the project's motto was always to see nothing, say nothing.

There were a few other kids in my class that couldn't read. My best friends–Jonathan and Ray–also struggled with school. If one in five students have dyslexia, the odds were they might have been experiencing some version of reading and writing struggles associated with dyslexia.

Jonathan had the best of everything and a loving family. He was very generous with everything he got, and sometimes it seemed as though he bought his friends. His parents were big-time drug dealers. They lived in a beautifully decorated home with Louis IV furniture, French antiques, and paintings from the 1600s. His dad was an older gentleman who was very well-respected in the community. We'd sometimes see him after school, and he would give us spending money.

At this point in my childhood, I saw Jonathan's dad as a well-dressed provider and a role model through my young eyes. I didn't question the 'how' or 'why' of the money my friend's dad doled out. Seeing Jonathan's relationship with his dad made me long to have my own father in my life. The brief encounters I had with his dad reminded me that I had never really spent time with mine.

I desperately needed my dad in my life. Although my father was around in my younger years, I did not have any genuine memories of him. I wanted to see how he walked and how he carried himself. As a young man, I had no one to identify with. I longed as a young boy to be held and loved. I needed someone to step in and save me. I guess I just needed an anchor and a clear direction. What I developed instead was wounded masculinity.

Not having my dad around when I needed him most was like a kick in the gut, a constant hurt inside that only added to my feelings of isolation. Not having a positive male role model left me more vulnerable to the realities of a learning difference. Not having a dad I could call my own placed an undue burden on my young sense of self. In the absence of a positive version of masculinity, I questioned who I was meant to be. However, instead of showing that hurt and confusion, my heart became more and more callous as I learned to be mean and brutal. I was subconsciously protecting myself from the pain of feeling abandoned. I would look to other males in the projects for an example of a workaround. If I wasn't able to handle school, how else could I belong?

Besides Jonathan, none of my friends in the projects had a dad. Without a father figure to look up to, we often emulated other men in the community or the media, even if they served as terrible examples. Without guidance, I learned by trial and error, with a lot of errors. The trails would come later. For me, the classroom would turn out to be just like the courtroom.

I remember the first time that I heard from my father. I was about nine years old. I was sitting on top of the kitchen counter when my mother unexpectedly handed me the phone. She told me that my dad wanted to speak to me. I stood there, frozen. Did I hear her right? Did she say my dad? A nervousness came over me because I was the first person he wanted to talk to. As my brother and sister stared, waiting for their turn, I wasn't sure what to say to this estranged man. "Dad?" I said for the first time. I did not actually understand what that meant, but I was just grinning ear to ear to be able to say those words to someone, finally.

I heard his voice on the phone. I couldn't believe the man on the line was actually *my* dad. He really existed! He did all of the talking because I was in total shock. "I miss you, son. You are my miracle child. That is why I gave you the name Ameer Baraka. 'Ameer' means 'king,' and 'Baraka' means 'charity giver,'" he explained. Even though I didn't comprehend much of what he said at the time, I hung on to his every word.

"When are you coming home?" I asked, hoping I would get to meet him in person soon. "I can't wait to meet you!" He never asked me about any personal details of my life, school, or education. But he promised that I'd see him soon. This was a lie. I would become all too familiar with his broken promises over the years to come.

"Why don't you tell me what you want for Christmas, so I can bring it for you when I see you? Do you know what you want?" my dad asked. I was so overwhelmed and excited by the question. My face lit up with anticipation. I had been watching many old westerns and cowboy movies late at night with my grandmother, and a guitar was the first thing that popped into my mind.

For months after that phone call, my mother had told me that if I continued to be good, I would get my guitar. My sister and brother were waiting to receive their gifts as well. As the days got closer to Christmas, Dash and I talked about the presents that our dad would bring. We were beyond excited.

"I can't wait to learn how to play the guitar," I'd say to Dash. "I'm gonna be really good, and I'll play for all the kids in the projects." I'd run around boasting and bragging to anyone who would listen. I told all the kids at school that I'd play music for them on the guitar that my dad was giving me for Christmas.

"Yea, Milly, I'm gonna jump all kinds of ramps on my new Huffy bike," Dash proclaimed. For weeks on end, we'd go back and forth on whose gifts would be better. Finally, we agreed to share, so we could both play with each other's presents. We talked about how we'd show off our gifts to all the other kids.

As Christmas approached, my mother told us about our dad not having enough money to buy our gifts. She sat Dash and me down and told us, "I want you guys to understand that your dad has been working hard to get your presents, but he wants me to tell you guys that he won't be able to get them in time for Christmas. He's run into some trouble and has to pay other bills, but he promised you will both get your bike and guitar after Christmas."

I could not believe the words coming out of her mouth. Disappointment washed over me. I was stunned with disbelief. How could this be happening? Why was this happening?

All my excitement and wild anticipation for Christmas were crushed. I thought about how embarrassing this was going to be. I had run my big mouth and told all the kids in the neighborhood, and at school, about the new guitar my dad was bringing me. I knew I'd be laughed at and made fun of, and I was not looking forward to facing the onslaught of teasing. That night, Dash and I cried together. Seeing my older brother so upset exacerbated how hurt I was feeling. Dad had done it again, let us down, and we were hurt and angry.

Early the next morning, I heard my grandmother's voice. "Why do you let Otis tell lies to those children? He's going to burn in hell," she said with boiling anger in her eyes and a voice that rang like thunder. I had no understanding of what 'hell' was, but whatever it was, according to my grandmother, my dad would suffer there. To a child like me, hell was a place saved for those who didn't give their children promised Christmas gifts. Maybe my dad knew hell was inevitable for him, so it didn't make a difference whether he got us the gifts or not. All we knew was we weren't important enough for him to be truthful and follow through. His words meant nothing.

"I know we are not getting the gifts, but is he at least still coming for Christmas?" I asked. "He's a seaman," my mother replied. "He's sailing around the world on a big boat." "Wow," I thought, "he must be rich if he is traveling around the world." But at the same time, I was confused. How could he have the money to travel the world but not send me my guitar? It just did not add up. None of this, my young world and the circumstances in it, made sense to me.

When my mother left the room, my grandmother looked me straight in the eye and told me the truth. "Your dad is in jail, Ameer," she exclaimed. "What's jail, Grandma?" I asked.

"A place where that nigga should be," my grandmother shouted without apology. I was even more confused with images of jail, hell, and a boat. If I could talk to him on the phone, why couldn't I see him? Why was he in jail? And how would I ever learn to impress other kids with music if I didn't have a guitar to play?

Chapter 3

PROJECT LIFE

When I was in second grade, I came home from school one day to stacks of moving boxes scattered all over the floor. My mother told us we were moving out of the projects and into a better place. At the time, I didn't want to move and leave all my friends behind. The projects were my home. Even though we practically moved across the street, it seemed like worlds away from the projects I had come to know.

My mother always wanted the best for us. "The projects are not a place to raise kids," she explained. "You'll get your own room and bathroom! There's even real carpet there." I didn't see why this was necessary because we all seemed to be doing just fine. I didn't care about having my own room or bathroom; I just wanted to be where all my life-long friends lived.

Soon after we moved, my mother met Charles, who came to live with us. Russhan and Dash stayed at my grandmother's house, so it was just my mom, her new boyfriend, and me. My mother always wanted a man around the house for me to look up to, even if he wasn't the best role model. Charles was a fun-loving guy, and I immediately took to him as a father figure. I was desperate, and he was nice enough to fill the void. Having him in my life was better than nothing, but he still couldn't fill the shoes of my birth father.

The three of us had so much fun together. Charles made me feel special and even loved. I'd light up with pride when he'd tell the guys on the corner that I was his son. I had always longed to have a man walk down the streets of the projects with me, arm and arm, and for him to call me his 'son.'

Loneliness is a feeling most fatherless young men are familiar with. At the time, I thought being with Charles felt the way it should; I liked being treated like a son. I idolized and appreciated him for that. Looking back now, as an adult, I realize he never talked about my school work or even asked what I wanted to be when I grew up. He was just *there*. Our time together was fun and games. He never instilled any values in me, never taught me what it was to be a man, never led by example, nor helped me set any healthy boundaries or contributed to my self-esteem. The one statement I remember him uttering was, "Be a man." What did that even mean, to be a man? I had no idea what that looked like, or the ideas I did have were completely misplaced. It would take me years to unravel what manhood was all about.

A friend of Charles' lived next door. He'd come over to smoke weed with Charles and my mother. One morning, I was home alone, and I heard the doorknob turning. I thought my mother was trying to get in. I approached the door as it swung open. Charles' friend was standing there with a knife in his hand. My heart stopped as I froze with fear, thinking he'd come in and kill me.

The man looked shocked and caught off guard to find me home alone. "Is your mother here?" he asked with his voice shaking slightly. "No… she just left…," I managed to say. I stared down at the long silver kitchen knife still pointed toward me. He took another look at me and walked away. I got ready for school, still shaken up, and left the house as quickly as possible.

When I got home that afternoon, I found my mother crying on the phone. All of her clothing, coats, the television, and stereo equipment were gone. I began to cry with her when I saw the disappointment in her eyes. She was a hardworking lady and did not deserve this. My grandmother had always taught us to watch out and be careful about the dangers of the projects. There was always robbing and killing around us, and clearly, crime had followed us outside the projects. My mom had thought we'd be safer here. I thought to myself, how could this happen living outside of the projects? I thought we'd moved here to be free of gang violence and get away from all that nonsense.

When I realized the strange events of that morning and the robbery might be related somehow, I decided to share it all with my mother and

Charles. "His friend came by this morning…" I started to tell them as I pointed at Charles. "When I opened the door, he was standing right there with a knife!"

Charles just looked at me blankly, without saying or doing a thing, as my mother yelled, "You need to go ask that, brotha! Did he break into my house? Go and see if my stuff is at his place!"

Charles was a coward and never confronted his friend. My mother was not the type to bring the police into our home or report a crime. Instead, we just moved again.

My mother and Charles broke up shortly after the break-in incident. She felt she needed a man who would stand up for us. So as quickly as he came into my life, Charles was gone. Thankfully, her next relationship, with Steve, didn't last long either.

Steve was as black as midnight. He was very tall, with broad shoulders and a large frame. I'd witnessed my grandmother be super protective of my sister Russhan. For a good reason, she never allowed her to hang around my mother's boyfriends. I still cannot fathom why she ever became comfortable enough with Steve to let her guard down.

Steve came around frequently and never really said much to Dash or me. He was noticeably drawn to Russhan and singled her out immediately by saying he always wanted a daughter. She was his little princess, and he always sat her on his lap to talk to her. Nowadays, there's a name for the way he treated my sister compared to my brother and me. He may have been 'grooming' Russhan from the moment he stepped through our door. I could not put my finger on his energy then, but something was creepy about Steve. I was glad he didn't stay around long.

The men who came in and out of my mother's life were never the men I should have been around. I was impressionable and seeking male attention. A sponge doesn't know what it's absorbing; it just soaks up whatever it's exposed to. Although most of her lovers were decent men, they too were probably raised without a father, which in part explains how they justified exposing me to their inappropriate lifestyle.

A man named Scooter came into the picture, and my mother seemed to genuinely love this guy. Scooter weighed all of a hundred-ten pounds, but he was still greatly feared within the neighborhood. He was a hustler and well known for shooting people. I'd go everywhere with him. Consequently, I began to see and participate in everything he was involved in.

Scooter was introduced to drugs at an early age. He would pass this lineage down to my brother and me. He began to take us to school on his ten-speed bike. Dash would sit on the handlebars while I'd be on the crossbars. I remember I had to hold bags of weed for him because he knew the police wouldn't search me if they stopped us. One day, he forgot to get the weed back from me when we got to our destination. I was at his mother's house, joyfully jumping on the bed with his nephews. The weed in my pocket fell out and burst open everywhere. I was terrified he'd be angry. But Scooter was cool about the whole thing and picked up the weed–just another day at grandma's house.

In that era of my childhood, I remember my mother had a big, bushy afro and wore large, round eyeglasses. It was the early eighties. She listened to Marvin Gaye, smoked weed, and vibed with her friends. Scooter kept a lot of weed at our house. Many people from the neighborhood would often drop in to buy weed, listen to music, and smoke. The grownups were too high to notice the kids were eavesdropping in the corner. I thought my mother's friends were cool. They talked about the Black Panther movement and how Blacks must continue to stay strong. I was overhearing important conversations that would shape my views on authority and race, not that they noticed.

Through their conversations, I overheard that both my dad and uncle were deeply rooted in the Black Panther organization. During their late-night discussions, I heard them say that there had to be snitches within the organization because the FBI frequently busted their meetings and took other brothers to jail.

When the adults were paying attention, look out. Scooter was a disciplinarian. One day, Scooter sent Dash and me to the store for ham to make sandwiches. Dash told the butcher to give us cheese instead of ham. I told the butcher that Scooter instructed us to get ham, not cheese, but my brother was older, so he chose to listen to Dash. When we got home, and Scooter saw all that cheese, he tore Dash up, 'real good.' Spankings were commonplace, and we definitely got our share.

When I was nine years old, my mother and Scooter had a baby they named Abdul Harris. I had finally become a big brother. I was too young to realize then what a responsibility that was. I couldn't have known what it was to be a good role model. All I knew was that I was no longer the baby in the family.

Scooter believed in education. While Dash excelled at school, I continued to do poorly. Scooter thought my mother's pacifying and babying me held me back academically. He gave me an ultimatum to improve my grades immediately, or there would be consequences. One day, Scooter knew I'd had a spelling test at school. He demanded to see how I did. Not surprisingly, I received a big, fat 'F' on the test. Knowing exactly where the paper was, I fake searched for it for about thirty minutes. As he entertained my mother in the kitchen, I was hoping that he'd forget about the test, but he didn't. He came into my room and sternly commanded, "Show me your test!"

After he saw how poorly I had done on the test, he took off his belt. I began yelling and screaming, hoping that my mother would intervene. After several licks, she came into the room, and he relented.

Especially at this age, I desperately needed guidance in my life. I also needed a trusted adult, or someone, anyone, to identify the root of my learning difference. What I did *not* need was to be punished for my inability to spell or to succeed in tasks I was failing to complete. With Scooter, unfortunately, there was always a beating for poor academic performance. When I needed someone to care more about the 'why,' I got punished instead. Why was I failing in school? My siblings were a testament to the fact that other kids in my family were able to study and learn. My dad may have been a hustler, but he was a smart one. My mom had gone to college. Yes, she'd dropped out, but she'd chosen to. Why was I different? My challenges couldn't be pinned on the 'nature' or 'nurture' argument.

Beating a child is never acceptable, but using corporal punishment to beat a kid who has no control over his academic achievement is an all too common and grossly misguided remedy. When I needed a velvet glove, I got an iron fist. The root cause of my academic failure would be left unattended, morphing into the root cause of my shame and, eventually, when I got older, other people's suffering.

To his credit, each night, Scooter would go over my homework with me. But I was never able to grasp any of it. I was challenged to understand or comprehend what I was reading. He couldn't have known why his efforts weren't helping. I'm sure many parents and guardians of children with learning differences think they're doing the right things to help their children. Experts don't call dyslexia an 'invisible disability' for nothing. Unlike being blind or deaf, dyslexic children aren't physically impaired in an obvious way. No one could see inside my brain. I could never write things down on paper the way the ideas were formulating in my mind. My thoughts were trapped, without a vehicle for self-expression.

Consequently, these thoughts never landed the way I wanted them to. My words were unable to be expressed. If I'd only learned to play guitar, maybe that would have been a language I could have understood and a way to express the creative energy that was always bubbling just under the surface.

Education lost its importance to me. I developed shame fatigue. I felt as if some invisible force held me behind. I couldn't and wouldn't abide by a constant barrage of negative feelings. I was made to feel angry, ashamed, and fearful. A child's brain cannot physiologically learn in a state of anxiety. My flight or fight chemistry had saturated my brain with high levels of cortisol, or stress hormones, for so long that I began to feel averse to the environment that made me feel the most stressed–school. Who could blame me?

At the beginning of winter in fourth grade, Scooter moved us to Atlanta, GA. My mother was much happier there, had a host of better job opportunities, and seemed to enjoy a change of pace.

Atlanta was very different from New Orleans. We spent a lot of time playing outside with our friends, just like we did in the projects, but getting to play in the snow and cold was a brand new experience. I had never seen snow in New Orleans. Life in Atlanta was pretty great, at least for a time.

After six months there, my grandmother began to miss us. She hopped on a train for a visit. It was nice to see her, eat her food and listen to her late-night stories. My grandmother had a sinking feeling, an intuition, that something was about to go wrong for us. She wanted us back in New Orleans. My grandmother left after her one-week visit. Dash cried like a baby. He loved my grandmother, and he missed her. I was a 'mama's boy.' If my mother was with me, I was always cool.

My grandmother kept persuading my mother to come back home to New Orleans. Three months later, she eventually gave in, left Scooter, and we moved back to New Orleans. My grandmother was relieved, and it was a great comfort to her to have us back. The only good thing about going home was I would no longer get beat up for failing my spelling tests.

A year later, the news was full of stories of kids being kidnapped and killed in our neighborhood back in Atlanta. Some of the older women in the projects thought we were 'blessed children' because we moved away just in time. My grandmother's intuition had been on target. She said God had his hands on us, and looking back at that time in our lives, I must agree.

Chapter 4

DEATH OF A BROTHER

Now that I was back in class with my good ol' friend Ray, life was all good again. The two of us shared the strong connection of struggling academically in school. We were also bonded over our love for Now and Laters and Jolly Rancher candies. He'd steal his mother's food stamps in order to keep us in a steady daily supply of candy.

We were in fifth grade, but neither of us attended class very often. We skipped school to go down by the canal. He'd show me the bruises on his body from his mother's beatings. I always knew when the beatings got really bad because Ray would be too embarrassed about his bruise marks and wouldn't show up for class. After school, I'd go down to the canal to find Ray and ensure he was okay.

Our fifth-grade teacher tried her best to help the students in her class (especially us boys), but there was only so much she could do. When Ray got in trouble and ended up in a juvenile detention center, 'juvie,' our teacher picked him up because his own mother didn't seem to care.

Ray did not show up to class for two weeks, and he was not at the canal where I usually found him. Our teacher knew we were close and asked me if I knew where he had been. I hadn't heard from him in a while. Running away was normal for him, so my eleven-year-old mind didn't think much of it.

I got home from school one day, and as usual, my grandmother was in the kitchen, cooking. The news caster's voice rose and fell in the background and mingled with the best southern cooking smells you can imagine.

Suddenly, I heard my grandmother's screams. "Oh my God," over and over. "It was Ray! It is Ray! They found his body!" she yelled as I ran as fast as I could into the kitchen.

I just stared at the screen, too shocked to move. As I watched in disbelief, they pulled my best friend's body out from the canal, miles away from where we lived. I couldn't believe it was true. My best friend was dead. My grandmother made me go to my room to stop watching any further. I slowly walked away and started to cry. I asked God why He would let this happen to Ray? Why did children have to die? The world wasn't safe. Ray wasn't looked after, and now he was dead.

This experience tore me apart. On the first day back in class, the whole class was in tears. Teachers checked up on me to ensure I was doing okay. They asked if I was having suicidal thoughts or wanted to kill myself because my best friend had drowned. I didn't want to talk to anyone.

Days and weeks went by. I hoped it might get easier, but it was still just as painful to think about as the day they discovered his body. No one talked about the stages of grief with me or explained how long that grief could last. I despised school before, but I hated that place even more now. I missed hanging out at the canal with Ray, laughing, playing, and catching tadpoles. We should've been in school, but like Huckleberry Finn's adventures, we were learning life skills that weren't being taught in school–plus, we had much more fun near the water, without structure, and without *books*. We also learned about the value of deep friendship. As we tested our freedom and anonymity, our bond only grew deeper outside the walls of public education.

That year was full of other great disappointments. On top of Ray's drowning, I had also failed fifth grade, which broke my mother's heart and made me feel totally incompetent. Russhan and Dash were doing so well in school. Why couldn't I catch on?

That whole summer, my grandmother kept me in front of the chalkboard. But her lessons still didn't work, and my spelling did not improve. I wish she'd known then that what she was writing and erasing on that board, how she saw letters and words, was light years away from how I saw them. Her teaching would never have registered with me. She couldn't have known that I needed an instructor who knew how to teach a targeted, systematic, specialized, phonics-based style program. I needed a reading specialist and a serious reading intervention. Anything less just wouldn't stick.

All those tears my mother shed didn't affect the eventual outcome. I just hated school. I felt terrible that I couldn't meet my mom and grandmother's expectations. I wanted to please them so badly. Instead, I internalized a sense of shame and blamed myself for failing. I was already making harsh judgments about myself. Even though I was only in fifth grade, my understanding of myself was that I was already a lost cause. I couldn't learn. Academic success seemed like an impossibility. I believed it was too late for me to learn to read or comprehend anything other than a resigned acceptance that I wasn't smart enough to stay in school.

The beatings and bribes or anything aimed at trying to get me to do well in school was utterly useless. The following school year, I had to go back to fifth grade. As you can imagine, that endeavor didn't go so well.

I was embarrassed about repeating a grade. Because I couldn't read, other kids laughed and made fun of me. I was now older and more conscious about how I was perceived. My hatred for school had only increased. I often cried like a baby without the soothing effects of milk or a swaddle. There was nothing to comfort and no one to protect me. I didn't feel any sense of security, and as a result, there was this growing sense of defiance–brewing like a slow storm churning out at sea, just waiting for the right wind to land on shore. The air inside me was primed for destruction. There was no chance in hell they were going to get me to learn a damn thing. I was conflicted, but I was also 'done.' I was done with the excruciating sensation that I was less than.

Considering I failed so many classes throughout elementary school, I still don't fully understand how I ever made it to junior high. I still couldn't read, and I hated every minute of my education. No one spoke of closing the achievement gap. No one addressed the trifecta of race, income, and education and the dangers of a community of disenfranchised youth with guns, drugs, and no money.

The most painful piece of the 'shame' puzzle for me, back then and to this day, was the reality of being neglected by my own family. Back then, our parents and educators didn't know what they didn't know. What's the excuse today? People still make heinous mistakes because they parent or teach the way they were parented or taught. Perhaps they themselves were undereducated or aren't able to see the root causes of their children or students' suffering. My peers certainly weren't taught to respect learning differences. No one knew enough to call my learning challenges what they were. There was no common verbiage that explained the reality of what I was experiencing–at least not in my household–and certainly not in the classroom.

My mother would ask me why I couldn't be 'smart' like my brother and sister. My family used 'dumb' and 'stupid' as my descriptors. I began to believe the onslaught of messaging that came at me like a series of sharp, emotional daggers from every direction. My internal narrative became a chain of hopeless thoughts and mistruths. Those self-beliefs began to spiral out of control. I never assumed that I'd finish school or be anything in life. I began to act the part. Acting out perpetuated what I perceived to be the truth of who I was.

When a new park called Pontchartrain Beach opened up that summer, my uncle took Dash and Russhan because *they* had passed their classes and moved on in school. I cried to go with them to no avail. I felt abandoned and alone. The actions of others reinforced my self-belief.

As I became bitter and frustrated, I took it out on other kids. In the projects, I became known for getting into fights. My behavior became so bad my family refused to take me anywhere in public. It was as if I would always be punished, as if I was not good enough for my own family. But it wasn't just my immediate family who were noticing my defiant behavior.

My older neighbors would tell my mother how I'd cursed them out. I'd run through the projects violently, like a wild-man, breaking bottles and windows or worse. I wanted to be better than my brother and sister in something, anything. If I could be better at being 'bad,' well, at least that was something I could call my own. My mother whipped my butt again and again, but that violent response to my behavior at home or grades in school only reinforced the pain I felt on the inside. Whoever thought fear was an effective substitute for unconditional love? Children don't misbehave for no reason, and the endless punishments couldn't change my situation. By then, I was growing bigger and taller. The ass whippings weren't as scary as they once were. The damage was already done by the time my mother and the other adults in my life stopped doling them out.

Chapter 5

FAILED MENTORS

My mother let me hang out with our neighbor, 'Big Man.' His business was legitimate, and he worked hard. But he was a liar and a cheat. He was like a mentor to me, *and* he taught me how to hustle. I enjoyed learning how to sell produce, fix cars, and cut grass. We made a lot of money together. But for as much as he taught me about supply, demand, and how to skim off the top, I was also a quick study on the hustle itself.

He was good at making things up, exaggerating everything, and always overpriced what he sold. "When you have a good product people want, you can demand the price they'll pay," he'd always say. This was a simple principle I later took with me into the drug trade.

The disciple eventually becomes the master. After a short while, I learned how to steal from him too. I'd charge the customers even more than we'd agreed upon and only give him what he thought the price was. He fired me when he found out, and I started doing business independently. I began mowing lawns (without a middle man). I loved the yards in the white, affluent, uptown neighborhoods. While cutting the grass, I'd steal anything I could get my hands on, something of value left lying around in the yards that I could sell to make money. I felt no remorse for stealing because it appeared these people had everything and wouldn't miss what I took from them. Rationalized thievery usually begins small and escalates.

I used my 'hard-earned' money to gamble. I loved playing dice. I'd play with some of the older boys on the block. I didn't realize it at the time, but they were beating me out of my money by using loaded dice. Everywhere around me, there was a hustle and cheating already in progress. One day the police came and broke up the dice game and mentioned that the dice were loaded. They split the money up and gave it to some of the kids who were watching us play. I couldn't believe how these older kids had tricked me and taken advantage of how young and gullible I was. Those are the lessons of the streets. You get hustled, and then you learn to be a better hustler.

Shortly after, a man named Bernie, who had just gotten out of prison, took me under his wing. I was a young teenager, and Bernie was about thirty-years-old. He was good-looking. He had long braids and a ripped body from working out every day during his five-year prison sentence.

People in the projects often had more respect for hardened criminals than those who had turned away from a life of crime. Men out of prison were respected in my neighborhood—as if they were college grads who'd just received a prestigious degree. Nobody in the projects messed with Bernie. Seeing this, I thought I'd be willing to go to prison to command the respect I observed he received wherever he went. I desperately wanted to be just like him, and he quickly became my criminal mentor.

I'd hear guys talk about how bad Bernie was in prison. He loved sharing his experiences about how he'd been able to knock guys out. Every day, I couldn't wait for school to be over. I walked through the toughest parts of the projects just to meet up with him. He'd drape his arm around my shoulder whenever we walked through the projects. Everyone saw he cared a lot about me, which made me someone. Hanging out with Bernie, who commanded so much fear and respect, made me feel special and important. I clung to his 'fatherly' attention and influence. I saw him as a 'real man.' I also thought that someday I'd be able to attract women the way he did. I was definitely coming of age and watching how attraction played out.

And then came Doe Doe. He also entered my life around sixth grade. He was a young hustler with a big personality. He was two years older, and he'd already dropped out of school. By the time he got to the eighth grade, he was already into multiple layers of criminal activity. He was known for getting into trouble for really trivial and stupid stuff.

I guess running away from my education pushed me closer toward a criminal lifestyle. It was not a conscious decision; it just seemed to happen that way. Street smarts led to street credibility, which led to criminal activity that brought home more money. In turn, minor crimes led to bigger crimes. Intergenerational poverty and addiction run like that. My legacy was already cast, and I played right into the hand I'd been dealt.

Doe Doe and I began smoking weed and started a spree of petty theft. His drug dealer cousin, Rod, didn't like Doe Doe because he was so ruthless. We'd spend all day at Rod's house just watching and waiting to see where he'd hide the money. After he'd leave, we'd break in and steal all his cash.

All the older guys I knew in our neighborhood carried a gun, so I felt like it was time for me to carry as well. In the hood, carrying a gun was a sign of respect and brought power. At that time in the projects, in the early eighties, killings were rampant–much more frequent than fights–murder was commonplace. Living the life I did, I wanted a weapon for protection and the power to stop a brother in his tracks if he happened to think he could mess with me.

I stole a 38-pistol from Doe Doe's cousin. One day, I saw him store the gun in the washing machine. Later, after he'd left the house, Doe Doe and I climbed back through the bathroom window and went directly to the laundry room to grab the gun.

The first time I held the gun in my hand, I knew that weapon would take me to places I didn't want to go. But after feeling the weight and gripping the barrel, I became one with it. A gun became an extension of me, my identity getting all intertwined with the cold, hard steel. No matter how I felt about myself or how much my mother and grandmother pressured me to do well at school, once I held that gun, there was no going back to the relentless effort school required. From this point forward, my innocence and childhood–or what was left of it–would disappear into the shadows of a dim street corner.

When the powerless find the object of their power, there's no turning back. Holding that weapon made the hopelessness I felt at school disappear. There was no way I was going to give up that feeling for the disempowered burden I had to endure every day in the classroom. Education seemed pointless. What I craved more than anything was respect and belonging—two things I could not find through academics.

Looking back decades later, I really should be dead. I was crazy wild back then, and I took too many risks with myself and other people's lives. I'd break into dope dealers' houses to steal their stuff without any remorse. Believe it or not, there was one thing I never allowed myself to do: steal from the poor. I only robbed those who I felt had enough to share. If I'd given myself a nickname in that era of my life, it would have been the "Robin Hood Hustler." That ethical boundary of not stealing from the poor helped me justify stealing in general. But something was still missing from my life, and no amount of thrill-seeking was going to fill the void. But that didn't stop us from trying anyway.

Doe Doe and I stole ourselves two fine pitbull puppies. Doe Doe named his puppy Sue, and I named mine 8-Ball. At four months old, these dogs were very vicious. Consequently, the girls at school feared us. We rarely went to class, but we brought our dogs to the front gate of James Derham Middle School during dismissal. Doe Doe loved to sick Sue on the young ladies. Our intimidation got so bad that we were banned from bringing our dogs to school anymore. I hate to think about the harm those dogs could have done to any of those students. We were obviously showing our dominance, or lack thereof, with the help of those powerful jaws. We had trained the dogs to be extensions of our own aggression. If respect wasn't in the cards, fear was our best substitute.

One rainy day, 8-Ball got sick. I didn't know what to do. One minute, she was throwing up the last bit of food she had left in her stomach, and the next, she took her last breath. Just like that, she was gone. Doe Doe's dog was in the kennel with 8-Ball when she passed. Sue seemed like she was trying to wake her up, and she cried out as if she could sense something was terribly wrong.

The rain was coming down heavy that day, and so were my tears. Her passing tore through me like an emotional knife. My grandmother always told me that God would not let anything bad happen to me. Then how could *He* let this happen? My memories from the day Ray was found at the canal came rushing back, crashing over me like so many waves of unprocessed grief. I was so mad at God that I started cursing him out. I wanted to blame someone. My grief turned to anger, then to rage.

When I told Doe Doe that 8-Ball had died, he simply shrugged and said, "Nigga, quit all that crying. We just gonna get you another one."

I quickly stole another dog from a new, cocky guy named Butch, who recently had moved to the hood. Butch was five years older and much stronger than me. I had no idea how, but he found out I had stolen his dog and paid me a visit the next day at school. He brought six guys from his crew with him. I had never seen any of these guys before. As they circled around me, my friends came to see what was going on. Butch said that he only wanted to fight me, one on one, because I was the one who stole his dog. I was reluctant to fight him. I knew that I would lose badly, and then my mom would whip my behind for fighting. I decided to rise to the occasion and face the fact that I had taken Butch's dog, and now I had to pay.

I had never experienced a beating like that. Every hit was a powerful blow right to my face. Butch knocked me down with the first punch. Once I was on the ground, he never let up, repeatedly punching my face and head. I tried to fight back, but he was too strong. I often carried my gun on me, but I never brought it to school. If the fight were in the projects, I would have used it on him. I guess God was protecting me that day because Butch found me at school–on one of those rare occasions I actually attended.

Butch's blood was boiling, and he didn't want to stop. My boys jumped on his crew to save me and ran them off the school grounds. My head was spinning, and my stomach was upset. I got up, and I was completely dazed. I immediately started feeling sick. I went to the principal's office, and they called my grandmother to pick me up. She took me to the hospital. The doctor checked me out and concluded that the fight caused a slight concussion.

When we returned home from the hospital, that stupid old dog I stole was waiting at the door. The beating wasn't worth it. I'd tried to repair my grief with a substitute dog only to resent that damn mutt altogether.

My grandmother was very upset with me. I got into fights frequently, but I'd never taken this bad of a beating. Dash and Russhan were good kids. This behavior was the opposite of what they'd do, and they certainly never came home with concussions. She always wished I could be just like my siblings, and this was another disappointment on her long list of ways I didn't match their abilities. She placed me in bed with a cold towel on my head. She said she'd send me to a boy's home for troubled young men if I didn't improve my behavior. I didn't pay attention to a word she said. I just wanted to lie down and feel better. I imagined putting my 38-caliber on Butch the next time I saw him.

Later, my mother came in from work to find me in bed with a concussion. She marched me straight to the car and drove to Butch's house. She wanted answers. Butch's mother was a very tall country lady. My mother got loud, and then Butch's mother got louder. I could tell that a fight was brewing. My mother wasn't walking away or backing down. Butch's mother realized how tough my mother could get, and she stepped back inside her house and shut the door.

Three days later, I went back to school. My friends wanted revenge, but with some time to think about what I did, I knew that I had paid the price of my poor decision. Butch was the best man that day. I had made a miscalculation and stolen the wrong dog.

That butt-whooping taught me it was time to start carrying a real gun. That was my takeaway. The 38-pistol that I stole from Doe Doe's cousin would not fire, so Bernie bought me a 32-handgun that held nine rounds. It was a nice pistol. And finally, it was mine.

Now that everybody knew I was strapped, my fighting days were over. No one even considered picking a fight with me because I always let them know, not so subtly, that I was packing heat.

Doe Doe and I hung out a lot on Jackson Street. All the families living there got along, and most were related. Everybody was a hustler; they either sold drugs or robbed people.

Doe Doe's mother always got complaints from the neighbors for our shenanigans. At about 6:30 am on Saturdays, Doe Doe and I would fly up and down Jackson Street on his dirt bike. All the families would threaten us. The two-stroke engine was loud, and they wanted us to leave the neighborhood in peace. Even in that rough neighborhood, it was a little too early for sunrise joy rides. We never thought about other people's needs. We simply did not care. We were young, rebellious, and invincible. Authority didn't matter anymore.

Even though we did not always care about what happened to other people, we always had each other's backs. One day, however, Doe Doe popped one too many wheelies on his motorbike, knowing he would hurt me. I got mad and started throwing punches at him. We got into a bad fistfight and didn't speak for a couple of days. I still went to his mother's house for breakfast that Saturday morning. She noticed that Doe Doe and I were not talking to each other. She told us that friends go through things sometimes, but we had to stick together. It didn't take us too long to fix things between us. We were still best friends. We shared a special bond *and* a mutual path to destruction.

Chapter 6

THE DRUG GAME

I was about fourteen and still in sixth grade when I had my first girlfriend, Tyra Lawson. She was the finest girl in the projects, with beautiful dark skin, beautiful teeth, and nice hair.

I don't even remember asking her to be my girlfriend. Somehow, it just happened, but not without adversity. She gave me her home phone number one day after I walked her home. When Tyra kissed me at the door, the kiss lightened my whole being. That kiss real kiss was something I had looked forward to for a long while. Each day I would meet up with her after school. The entire neighborhood knew that I was finally in with a beautiful young lady. My status had grown by association, and I knew it.

We were in the same English class, which I hated. One day in class, I will never forget, I sat in the back row (as always) and opened my textbook, trying to avoid being called on to read. Tyra walked in and sat down at the seat next to me.

I was horrified when the teacher called on me to read the chapter. Tyra smiled at me with confidence. I guess she thought that her boyfriend would read the passage without difficulty. I didn't know any of the words on the page and the teacher had to help me with every single word. I felt hopeless and enraged. I wanted to run out of the classroom and just disappear. I had never felt that level of embarrassment in my life. I didn't call Tyra after that day, and just like that, we were done.

I lost more than my first love that day; it was a tipping point in my life. I knew I was never coming back to school. This was the last straw. I lost all desire to be there, even for sports or the more social aspects school brought. I began passing up the chance to be with other kids my own age. A new, dark chapter opened up in my life. It was time to be a dope dealer. Time to drop out and tune out the noise of shame.

My mind was made up already. My mother and grandmother couldn't force me to attend school by spanking me any longer. I was physically already a big kid. My mother brought me to school, and as soon as she left, so did I. There was nothing they could do to stop me from defiance. I was already lost in the system, and no one was willing or able to find me, especially if I decided not to be found.

My desire to go to school vanished. After repeating third, fifth, and seventh grades, I had lost my buy-in. In my young mind, school felt like a repressive system of education that kept holding me back and pushing me down. I did not have one teacher who flagged me for a learning difference. I wasn't screened or tested, not once. Not having any skills in the classroom hurt me. My life was increasingly hijacked by bad behavior, and I felt messed up. Now, I was a fourteen-year-old kid who hated school and couldn't read. The vicious cycle I was in got smaller and smaller, and I felt like I was attracting more of the very things I didn't want: violence, drugs, and a self-perpetuating cycle of cause and effect. I don't know how I got through junior high. I never passed any tests. I had all Fs on my report cards, yet for many years (when I wasn't held back), I still went on to pass to the next grade. Nobody cared that I couldn't read. Or, perhaps, my teachers weren't trained to detect the glaring reality head-on or how and when to intervene.

Looking out of the project windows, I felt so uninspired. Kids would be playing in the courtyard, unaware that this could be their final destination in life. No one told us that life could be bigger and better than this. No one spoke of the tools we'd need to escape the statistics of incarceration. I was a young black male living in one of the most violent neighborhoods in the country, *and* I was unknowingly dyslexic. Maybe the adults in our lives couldn't see the possibility of more or what could exist beyond the confines of our asphalt and concrete reality. Growing up in the projects robbed us of any other perspective. Marian Wright Edelman, Founder and President of the Children's Defense Fund, once said, "You can't be what you can't see."

I used to think if there was a God, why let this be? Why let this be my life? Every night, my grandmother and I would pray and ask him to help us get the things we needed. Our prayers were left unanswered, and we kept on struggling for our basic survival. Why would God let us, me and my siblings and our friends, grow up poor and uneducated? In all his omnipotence, how couldn't He foresee all the destruction happening in so many parts of the projects and so many poor neighborhoods in cities across the country or the world? Most of us grew up with purgatory as our backdrop. If you fear you'll be shot when you step out your front door, that's a form of hell. I can see the contributing factors now, but back then, all I felt was the sheer desperation of a black boy with no future. The systemic ways humans learn to be cruel to one another originate in our education system—or lack thereof. Suffering begets suffering.

I felt that selling dope was my only hope of ever having anything of value in my life. Before I knew I had a choice, or a voice, to advocate for myself, I succumbed to a life of drug dealing. Selling drugs didn't require me to read. I knew most of the guys selling drugs couldn't read either. I was good at math, and I just needed to count stacks of hundreds. If one in five children have dyslexia, the chances of these guys also having a learning difference was pretty high. I wanted to be part of that gang. I could be good at entrepreneurial pursuits, even if they were illegal. Most dyslexics are really skilled at finding workarounds. This would be mine.

Doe Doe introduced me to all of the players in the drug game. He was already well connected and had the needed personality traits: short on empathy and impulsive. Many of my friends advised me to hang out with someone with a better reputation. But I had nowhere better to be than in the game, and I had no better way of getting in the game than palling around with Doe Doe.

I was fourteen when I began delivering cocaine for Mike B. He was a low-key guy in the hood and highly respected in the drug world. He had previously seen me in a fight on the basketball court with a boy much bigger than me. I hadn't backed down. Mike approached me, saying he needed a 'little nigga' like me who didn't get scared easily. Since I was still a kid, he knew that the cops would not suspect me as a drug dealer.

Mike, at age thirty-eight, had the drug game on lock. People from all over New Orleans respected this guy. His drugs were the cleanest, not as cut with as many other substances as some of our more greedy competitors. The drugs he sold were just the way he got them. Other guys on the block, who had been trying to enter the dope game, were mad that I was already part of Mike's trusted inner circle. Everyone wanted to get close to him, but he chose me.

Mike's parents loved me. They ensured my stomach was always full and that Mike took good care of me. Mike made sure I didn't have to compete with anyone else. I had the best dope (less cut cocaine) and the biggest bags. Many brothers in the game would buy coke and mix it in a plain white powder to dilute the strength and try to make more money. We didn't do that and were able to move large quantities of product fast.

Mike had always told me about quick flips. He said, "You never want to be out on the streets too long selling your coke. The best way to sell is to be the one selling the purest grade so that you can get rid of your bags quickly. That way, the police won't have to see you out there all day, every day. You go out for a few hours at a time, and everybody knows your stuff is the best, and they buy from you." Quick and easy.

As the drug dealer, Mike didn't sell on the streets. He kept a low profile to avoid running into the cops. As his runner, I handled the hand-to-hand transactions and returned the money to him. Sometimes I kept the dope on me, and other times, I stashed it out in the project's hallway for 'safekeeping.'

I'll never forget my first dope sale. The entire process was exhilarating. Ducky was a runner in the projects too. He was also an addict and hoped to end up with a free bag (or two) of cocaine at the end of his day of sales. Even without much money of his own, he secured a steady supply of drugs to support his own habit by being a runner. He confided one day that I needed to have a safe place to hide my dope. Somehow he knew the police were getting suspicious, and he warned me not to carry any drugs with me. I kept the stash far enough away from me so that if the police found it, I wouldn't get charged for possession.

When a customer came, Ducky whistled to me and held up his two fingers. I grabbed two bags from my stash. He came over with thirty dollars and picked up the bags to hand to his customer. I was finally 'officially' in the drug trade. My heart pounded, and my hands were sweating. I was nervous yet also thrilled beyond imagining. I couldn't believe I was finally selling drugs. ~~When the money touched my hand, all the fear melted away, and I felt like a real man.~~ I had arrived. ~~I didn't have to depend on anyone for money anymore.~~ I ~~didn't have to pray to God for help to support my family.~~ *I* could help get us ~~out of poverty.~~ After all, as the most commonly misquoted, non-biblical saying goes, "God helps those who help themselves."

That summer, when no one else was home, I began selling drugs in our backyard. I earned a thousand dollars within a few hours. I sold fifteen-dollar bags of cocaine and made more money in a few hours than most skilled workers made in a week. Mike was excited about my growth potential and told me I could make way more than that.

I also snorted my first line of cocaine that summer. Mike and I were in his room preparing bags of coke for a drop-off. Mike always tested a bit of his supply to check the quality. This time, he offered me a line–right off the scale, off the corner of an ace of spades playing card. I felt like this single act was a rite of passage. I was actively facing my own mortality every day. Why not feel what others were paying us to feel? A validated sense arose inside me. The change in identity I was craving suddenly flourished. That first line of cocaine up my nose legitimized me in some important way I couldn't fully grasp. ~~A snort of coke made me see myself as a man.~~ I thought that now, I could live up to the expectations of real niggas and the other drug dealers I knew. I finally felt like I fully belonged, and the disappointments of all the failed expectations around schooling completely disappeared. I had a new identity now, and I liked how that felt. I felt capable and mature. The crippling doubt and shame were gone and in their place was a new sense of possibility.

That first snort was a rush I had never felt before. All of a sudden, it was as if the drug cracked open my head and obliterated all the negativity residing there. I heard a clear bell ring in my brain. After about ten minutes, a bad taste came down my throat. Mike told me to chill out; it was just the coke draining out of my nose. This post-nasal drip tasted terrible and burned. I didn't like the sensation in my throat, but I embraced the feeling in my brain.

When the packages were all ready, I began my deliveries. No other kids my age were snorting coke–just Doe Doe, one other kid we knew, and me.

I felt bright and energetic. My senses were keen and alert. I had never felt this great, and I knew I wanted more. I felt more confident and sure of myself. I had the coke and Mike B. to thank for that.

I had strong backers in the drug game and the hood. Without much effort, I found myself at the top of the food chain. Therefore, not many people ever tried to screw me over. One must have a powerful team and at least a few allies to be respected. The criminal pecking order, especially in the drug trade, seems universal. One rarely gets messed with when they have a mighty army behind them. Mike was the general of my strong army. He would get anyone killed if they bothered him or any of *his* people.

One day, while talking to a couple of guys on the porch, I made a rookie mistake. For just a split second, I took my eyes off my stash. Ducky had snuck up and tried to steal my entire stash. I noticed him out of the corner of my eye and ran towards him–full speed. I went off and thought about killing him. "I will shoot your brains out if you ever try to do that again," I yelled.

Ducky tried to laugh it off, but I was serious. When Mike learned about the incident, he told Ducky never to mess with me again. Even though Ducky was twenty years older than me, he had to respect me because he respected Mike. This was drug dealing 101. There was a hierarchy, and one needed to learn one's place in it–both to be protected and to profit.

People respected me enough that if I needed anything, they had my back. Even though I was just fourteen, I was frequently told that I'd be a big-time cocaine dealer someday. These early sentiments about my abilities and potential would make me pursue the drug life with ever increasing drive and passion. I thought I was exactly where I belonged, which only added to my desire to be the best at what I did.

By now, my respect was growing, and people were becoming increasingly jealous of me. I was on top of the world. I was achieving greatness and finally succeeding at being the best at something.

My name was becoming well-known in the drug scene of New Orleans. I began taking short trips to Miami or Houston to score cheaper kilos of cocaine. As the money flow got stronger, so did my cocaine habit. Some days, if I had five or even eight bags left over after a day of selling, I'd just snort the rest of my stash.

One day, Mike put out a hit for a guy in another project who had snitched to the cops. Four of Mike's guys were preparing for the kill, and they needed another gun. I ran home and got my 32-revolver, which I had purchased for just twenty dollars from another desperate cocaine addict. I wanted to be bad and tough and be included in the mission to punish the snitch. I pleaded to go along and be part of the action. Mike and his crew refused to let me in the car because I was too young, and they wanted to protect me.

'Pop' was one of New Orleans's most feared killers. He, too, was from the Calliope projects, where we lived. I was cool with him, but he didn't like Doe Doe. One day, about five of us were sitting on the porch, including Doe Doe, when Pop started talking smack. "Doe Doe came around the hood the other day with some bell-bottom slacks and ugly-ass shoes," he smirked. Pop tried to get me to go along with him, "Milly, tell Mike and Terrell about Doe Doe and them bum-ass shoes."

Doe Doe was my best friend, and I didn't join Pop in trying to humiliate him in front of the other guys. When Doe Doe had taken enough of Pop's abuse, he left the porch. Pop became angry with me for not agreeing with him. I had somehow, inadvertently, offended Pop's sense of the hierarchy. My refusal to call out my friend on his fashion choices was an affront to Pop's sense of loyalty. I had failed his test by not agreeing with him.

Toxic masculinity was the norm, not the exception. We were operating out of our reptilian brains. The pecking order was constantly being challenged, and there was always a reshuffling of who was on top. Nonchalantly, Pop walked up behind me and stood on the stairs. Suddenly, I felt his shoe kick me in the back of the head. I knew Mike would never respect me if I just sat there and did nothing. He didn't interfere either. I was a man, and I had to stand up for myself. I turned around and started yelling. "What'd you do that for? I'm going to kick your ass." Pop yelled back, "Nigga, you gonna try to fight me back?" Even though I was scared, I threw the first punch. Pop swung back and hit me right in the face.

Pop was known for shooting people, but his fighting skills were limited. When I realized that I could actually beat him, my fear melted away. My strength was out of his control. I just hoped he wouldn't shoot me. We went at it for about twenty minutes, and he finally wore out. Everybody saw him get torn up, and once again, I had proved myself as a man. I hadn't shown fear. I had gone through hand-to-hand combat without giving in to my hesitation.

As I walked home, I could see the joy in the eyes of those who had witnessed the fight. They were smiling at me, letting me know that they were glad I had stood up to him and beat him up. I had taken on *the* most feared guy in the projects only to show him up. There was a small thought in the back of my mind that maybe he would retaliate and try to kill me. But I knew I was too young for him to mess with, and I hoped that Mike and the crew would back me up.

After that day, people looked up to me. I capitalized on my new social collateral. I felt like people 'loved' me, and I could get away with even more. I started stealing other people's dope and running brothers who trespassed (from other parts of the projects) out of my neighborhood. I began doing the same kind of stuff Pop was known to do. There was a change in the guard. I was defending my territory and putting my own stake in the ground. I was not someone to be messed with.

Chapter 7

HOPELESS

As a kid, my grandmother had us pray before bed. Dash and I always joked around while praying. My grandmother kept a belt under the bed and often threatened us with it.

Dash wanted to be a professional football player, and he trained hard for his dream career in the NFL. I was planning to make a living selling drugs. My training was smoking the best weed and rubbing elbows with the most successful dope dealers in the neighborhood. I never gave a single thought to my little brother Abdul. I never thought that at five years old, he was watching everything I did and listening and hanging on every word.

While most kids dreamt of becoming the next Michael Jordan or Tom Brady, I dreamt of building playgrounds for kids and helping them get through school. I envisioned ways for kids to have positive things to do in the hood and planned to finance this vision through selling drugs. Based on my experiences as a kid, all we had access to was trouble. When I used to steal stuff from white neighborhoods, I saw the swings and well-maintained parks with envy. I wondered why we couldn't have access to those things too. My faith in this dream was unshakable.

For me, being around Mike was equivalent to being around a star athlete. He was my hero, and I idolized him. With no positive role model, and unbeknownst to my grandmother, I prayed to become a big-time dope dealer. I wanted to give back to my family and build up my community by helping others live better lives. I didn't care where the money came from; I just wanted to help people out of poverty.

My mother and grandmother thought Mike was a good guy and let me hang around him. Mike held my money because my mother would have had a nervous breakdown if she had found out what her son was up to. Money was coming in so fast, and I was more than ready to spend it–think Bally lizard-skin shoes, Calvin Klein, Members Only jackets, Polos, and brand new Adidas. Clothing and shoes I could have never afforded until now made up my everyday wardrobe.

Eventually, my family found out about my new lifestyle and sat me down in the living room. With tears and disappointment in their eyes, my mother expressed how badly she wanted me to go back to school and get my life back on track. My grandmother kept saying I was too young to be involved in all the stuff she had heard about.

I knew I had to deny everything because I didn't want them to worry about my dangerous lifestyle. I insisted that I wasn't selling drugs and what they heard was all a big lie. They also wondered if drug money was funding my new wardrobe. I told them that Mike was a benefactor, giving me money and buying things for me because he wanted me to have a better life. They weren't buying what I was trying to sell. What I couldn't say to them was that I felt too good to give up what I was doing. I had taken my life into my own hands, and nothing they could say or do would prevent me from enjoying some of the finer things in life. I had clout and designer clothes–a teenager's dream and difficult to argue with.

My grandmother just sat there crying, calling upon the name of Jesus and praying he'd help me. It hurt me to cause them so much pain. But I was already too embedded in the drug world to get out. Plus, I didn't *want* to get out. At this point, I had no skills or desire to do anything else. I knew this was my only realistic future. Besides, I had big hopes for myself to become a successful dealer.

Once things settled down, I walked out of the house and headed toward my drug-selling spot. I lit up a joint to ease my mind and escape the pain of what had just happened at home.

When I got to the end of the projects, I ran into Pop. He jumped out of his car and headed towards the guys standing on the corner. He proudly bragged that he locked both his girlfriends inside the trunk when they refused to give in to his sexual demands. I knew both of the women in the trunk, and I felt terrible for them. I could hear both of them crying, begging him to let them out. I knew if I helped them, Pop would have killed me, so I just kept my mouth shut. Hear nothing, see nothing, do nothing.

Many of my friends thought that this was how men treated and controlled women. A few of the guys started to laugh, maybe because they thought they had to, or perhaps they were just as screwed up as Pop. I didn't think it was funny. I'd never want something like that to happen to my sister. I couldn't take hearing those women crying, so I just turned around and walked away. That's the street code in the projects. Even though we knew it was wrong, we just looked the other way.

Those women must have feared for their lives and could not get out of the relationship. They knew Pop was dating both of them simultaneously, but they were too scared to do anything that might upset him and get them killed. I had met one of the women before. After a while, I could see Pop had crushed her pride and self-esteem. I used to see her roaming the streets, confused about life. A few days later, I heard that Pop had poured scalding water on her. She was rushed to the hospital with twenty percent of her body covered in severe burns. Pop was Satan himself or utterly possessed by him.

Pop was finally arrested after he severely beat his girlfriend in her own mother's house. The woman's mother wasn't having it and called the cops. The incident was all over the news. The police weren't trained to recognize domestic violence when they saw it, or perhaps she was too terrified to press charges. Pop was out of jail, fast.

The violence was constant and brutal. The first time someone shot at me was when I had jacked a Rolex from a guy who had just finished a burglary. I punched him in the face, grabbed it, and walked off. Later that night, he saw me walking around the projects. I heard the sound of motorbikes coming up on me from behind. I heard gunfire and realized the gun was pointed in my direction. Suddenly bullets whizzed by my head, just barely missing me. I was not scared at first because people shoot guns in the projects all the time. However, I suddenly realized I was the target when I saw who the shooter was. I wished to make it home to get my gun, but there was no time for that, so I began to run as they chased me on their motorbikes. I ran into a dark area with no lights. Sitting behind an old car, I heard them slowly pass me. I held my breath, hoping they would keep going and not find me.

When they were out of earshot, I slowly got up and tried to leave, but I heard their motorbikes turn around and come back. I crept back to my hiding spot. I was still just a kid, but I had gotten myself into a big, life-and-death mess.

Things get real when we come face to face with death. Those guys were trying to kill me that night, and I knew I'd had a close call. My grandmother and mother's words ran through my head. God was looking over me that night. I did not get shot, and I was still alive. I wish the incident had scared me enough to switch gears, but it didn't.

I had never shot anyone with a real gun, but that night I wanted to. It meant being a real gangster. I wanted to get that respect, and I knew this was my chance. Perhaps the value of human life didn't translate to a kid who'd grown up with death on his doorstep. I ran straight to a friend's house nearby. "I need a gun! Niggas are trying to kill me," I panted when he opened the door. Without hesitation, he reached into his shirt and handed me his 357-Magnum. "Go take care of business," he said.

I went back to the projects and saw their motorbikes parked in the grass by their building. I snuck around the corner where the guys were hanging out on their porch, just across the street from me. The guy who'd shot at me walked out of the building onto the front porch and stood right in my line of sight. I was positioned on the opposite side of the street, thirty yards across from him. I thought to myself, this is it. I had him now.

While gripping my 357-Magnum, I felt no fear, just complete control, and power. I rationalized my decision saying they shot at me first, and now I was going to take care of them. I didn't care who was on that porch with them; if they were innocent bystanders or part of the crew who'd chased me, they were going to get it now.

I cocked back the hammer of that 357 and pulled the trigger. I shot twice. When I hit one of the guys in the stomach, I began running backward while still firing the gun toward the group. They started shooting back, and I was dodging a storm of bullets. Neighbors on nearby porches began to run and scream, everyone shouting for their kids to come inside.

The muzzle blast, the explosion of fire that came out of that 357 was like lightning. I felt an incredible adrenaline rush every time I pulled the trigger. I was amazed at the power in my hand and the authority it gave me.

I had already used four of my six rounds. I needed to save at least two in case they got behind me. I ran away through the projects, and they didn't follow. Part of the thrill was just knowing I had gotten away with my retribution, completely unharmed.

When I returned his gun, my friend asked, "Is the nigga dead?" I replied, "No, but I know for sure I hit one of them." He told me to go inside and chill for a bit. I sat down with no worry, no thoughts of cops or somehow getting caught. Maybe it was the adrenaline or naive hubris, but I wasn't even scared.

Two days later, a guy named Meatball shot Doe Doe in the leg and stomach. While visiting Doe Doe in the hospital, I recognized the guy I had shot, lying three beds down. When he saw me, we thought he'd give the doctor my name, so Doe Doe told me to get out of there.

After that close encounter with death, I reevaluated my feelings about the gangster life. I knew life in prison wasn't what I wanted. I was still selling drugs, but I needed to make some immediate changes if I wanted to make my life any better.

My mother registered me for school in another school district, far away from the projects. I gave school one more honest chance, but it lasted only briefly. I still couldn't read and wasn't motivated to do any school work. To use a mixed metaphor: you can lead a dyslexic back to school, but you can't make him read. When my mother dropped me off at my new school, I simply took a cab right back to the projects. If I stayed on campus, I sold stolen goods (for double the price) or found younger guys to sell dope for me.

The truth was, I was too far behind academically and too addicted to my gangster lifestyle to make any real change. At this juncture, education was the farthest thing from my mind. Teachers wondered why I didn't take school seriously? If they only knew how much I wanted to do well academically and how incapable I felt of achieving even a semblance of grade-level skills. I wasn't just in the weeds, I had already drowned. If someone had figured out my academic profile at some point in K-3, I might have had a chance. By the time I reached high school, it was beyond too late. I hadn't just fallen completely through the cracks of academic failure; I had disappeared entirely. They couldn't see me, and I wanted to be invisible.

Chapter 8

MURDER, MURDER, MURDER

I left school early on Fridays to sell dope because that was the most profitable day on the streets. No one was out because it was rainy, cold, and damp that morning. A guy named Tim from another project was selling cocaine in my hood. He stepped on my turf, which didn't sit well with me. The 'old timers' taught me never to allow dudes from another area to sell drugs in my hood. The top guys never let such things happen.

I walked up to him and asked, "What are you here selling?" "Coke," he replied. "You know that you can't sell anything in this project because you're not from back here, nigga."

"Back off. This ain't your project," Tim growled. We both paused. The tension was palpable and kept building between us. He knew what I had just said was a *not* so veiled threat. Game on. He was stronger than me, and his first punch landed square in my face. We fought and rolled around in the mud until we were both worn out and tired. I told him again, "Don't be here when I get back."

I was going to defend my hood and my manhood. He'd disrespected me and the street code when he'd dared to come sell on my turf. I walked to the other side of the projects and told my sister's boyfriend to give me the 357-Magnum he kept in his car. I planned to use it on Tim, not to kill him, but just to put a few holes in him in order to teach him a lesson. I actually thought bullets were a good way to communicate.

Tim went upstairs to his cousin's house. I waited for him to come back down the stairs into clear view. I wasn't nervous or second guessing myself.

I had already shot a gun before and knew its power. He came down the stairs in what seemed like slow motion. I didn't think he had a gun until he came outside. He began firing at me first, shooting across the courtyard some forty yards away.

The rain poured, and it felt as though the temperature had dropped to zero. Everything seemed to slow down. I knew this duel had devolved into a full on shoot-out. I was just shooting into the night. I had no intention of actually killing him. My whole motivation was rooted in gaining respect, not inflicting death. I knew Tim was not aiming for me either. I don't know what invisible force possessed me in that particular moment, but suddenly, I raised my gun and pointed it directly at him. I fired several more times, this time with concerted aim. The discharge lifted my hand with each shot.

My last shot hit him in the chin. I could see his brain as it blew out just before he staggered backward and collapsed. His gun fell out of his hand and hit the porch. I ran over to see if he was dead. I knew I had to finish him off if he wasn't. That was how things were done. If I had learned nothing, it was to leave no witnesses. I had to make sure that he didn't tell the police or later identify me. There seemed always to be motivation to seek revenge, but usually, you brought your friends to help with payback. I was alone, and he was half dead.

As I stood over him, his eyes were wide open and full of fear. He was struggling to breathe, and his body was still moving and twitching in quick spasms. I knew at that moment that this man was going to die. My heart was racing. The heinous act of taking a life was the most surreal moment I'd ever experienced. There was no turning back. I had crossed over and bypassed an essential part of my own humanity by robbing someone else of theirs.

Tim's cousin watched the whole thing from his third-floor window. He began hollering at me and crying with the rage and grief of loss. I ran back to my sister's boyfriend's car, and we drove to his house in record time. On the way there, over the car radio, I heard about a deadly shooting that had just occurred in the Calliope projects. How strange to hear of a news report all about a murder and know who'd been directly responsible. There would be no escape from knowing the grizzly details of this man's death. I could not hide the reality of what I'd just done from myself.

During the twenty-minute drive, my grandmother's words repeatedly played in my head, "Thou shall not kill." According to what she had preached my entire growing up, I knew I was destined for hell. The scriptures were quite clear on this point.

I felt an overwhelming fear of getting caught, but somehow, I felt safe once I got to my sister's boyfriend's house. I had a fake smirk on my face. Perhaps I thought if I feigned confidence, I could quell a growing sense of dread that lay just underneath the surface. I had taken a man's life–something I could never give back. What about his family?

My sleep was marred by those thoughts each night. I kept replaying what happened and wondering if I could have shot him in the leg instead. If I had only aimed lower, maybe I wouldn't have killed him. I cried like a baby. I kept picturing how my grandmother described hell. Every night, the nightmare images of eternal, burning pires continued to haunt me. My grandmother said that God told her in a dream that I had killed a man. Of course, I denied it all. I felt even more guilty for accusing her of being a liar. I stopped selling drugs for a short period and stayed low at my sister's boyfriend's house.

Next, I moved into Mike's apartment. Mike told my mother and grand-mother that I'd be staying with him for a while. They still approved of Mike. The other guys who came in and out of Mike's place would tell me what a great job I did. However, I no longer needed other people's approval. I realized that I was a man now. I also understood too late, I hadn't needed to kill someone to prove that.

I told Mike about my nightmares. His remedy was to give me more dope to help me escape my demons. I couldn't sleep or eat. All I did was smoke weed and snort cocaine.

At just fifteen, my life was spiraling out of control. I had killed a man, and I was on the run. I was a dope fiend, a full-on addict, snorting about three grams of cocaine a day. I felt like I lived in the twilight zone. Nothing was real. I am not even sure how I survived those months. I always forgot to lock the door, left stuff all over the house, and couldn't remember anything. Day upon day passed. I was so coked out of my mind and didn't even care. I was becoming a major liability to Mike, so he finally kicked me out of his place.

My sister's boyfriend let me move back in with him. Meatball was also in hiding there as well because he had just killed a guy. He'd walk around with a blanket on his head, shades on, smoking crack all night and listening to hardcore rap music.

I wasn't on the streets, selling. Still, things were rapidly moving from bad to worse. Living with these guys meant all I heard all day was talk of people they'd killed or planned to kill. I felt my moral conscience diminishing with each passing day. The drug that at first liberated my mind and made me feel so clear and focused ultimately had hardened my heart and sent my life into a downward spiral. I was desensitized to everything, including pain and any semblance of joy. I felt like I had lost my soul. I was a shell of a human, and I simply didn't care about anything anymore.

Even though I knew it was wrong, thinking about killing someone again didn't bother me. Being surrounded by all this violence and so strung out on drugs, I lost my power to choose to be different, choose the good path, or make different choices. Cocaine had hijacked my nervous system, made my teenage brain more aggressive, arrogant, and impulsive, and directly contributed to my violent crime. I was numb and certainly could not see my destructive behavior through the cocaine veil.

Kids my age, still in school, were enjoying their lives the way they should. Most of their focus was on passing a test or getting their driver's license. All the while, here I was, a body inundated with drugs; in so deep, there was no way to change back to who I'd been or focus on the childhood concerns I'd long since abandoned.

Two months later, when I needed money, I had nowhere else to turn but the streets. Since I was back in the drug game, I eased up a bit on my own drug habit. I had to slow down my violent thoughts. I felt better and, for a brief period, decided never to kill unless my life depended on it. Word got out that I was back in the dope game. Tim's brother and father were looking for revenge. I started carrying a bigger gun–a 44-magnum.

I planned to kill both of these men if they approached me. If I happened to see them before they could get to me, I'd be ready. That was the mentality– outgun the people who were after you for being after them. Revenge killings were just standard practice. That's how devolved this game was. Kill or be killed. The weak risked being dead. I wouldn't have my mother standing over my casket crying, so I decided then and there—I'd rather be judged by twelve than carried by six.

I was the first and youngest in my hood to kill another man. After that, it seemed everyone started killing. Bee, a young guy who sold my dope while in school, was also eager to kill. He killed a man who he said was trying to kill him. A common defense, but I didn't believe him. I think he killed to earn the respect he saw I had gained—a copycat killer, if you will.

His brother, Carlos, killed without remorse. Even so, everybody loved Carlos. He was a cool, little guy, quiet and nice looking. But once I started giving him cocaine, he went absolutely berserk. One day, Carlos and I robbed a store. When I witnessed him shooting the owner, I took off and ran, the whole time thinking, "Why did he do that?" I learned later that he had gone through the register and the store owner's pockets. He had walked away with ten thousand dollars in cash, and he'd kept it all to himself.

A month later, Carlos killed a drug dealer from the ninth ward, which was almost as rough of a place as the third ward, where I lived. Carlos shot him when the dealer refused to hand Carlos some of his flashy jewelry. Even though the dealer ended up giving Carlos everything, he was left in the streets and bled out.

If a guy had come up and threatened me with a gun in those days, I'd have given him the shirt off my back or anything shiny I had that he wanted. A guy can always get another shirt, but a guy cannot get another life once he's dead. This third ward dealer should have known the street code of never wandering into another hood draped in jewelry. Rule number one: do not wear jewelry in places you do not know anyone. Rule number two: if someone pulls a gun and asks for your stuff, just give it up. This guy died for nothing but the pride of not being robbed of a gold chain. The senselessness of death was all around us. To say death was 'normal' on our streets is to point out how little lives were worth.

Everyone knew Mr. Smith, our ice cream truck driver. He was a white guy who loved black kids and always told us we were the strongest children on the planet. He would often hand out cones as he taught us about black history, our history. Up until then, I had always thought black people were just enslaved people from the past, but Mr. Smith explained it differently. "Africa was and still is the richest place in the world."

Mr. Smith always kept his money bag in the truck. Bee was planning to rob him. I told Bee that it wasn't worth the few hundred dollars he'd get if he knocked off that ice cream truck. But Bee didn't listen. Mr. Smith got shot four times over a few hundred dollars. He put himself in harm's way to improve our lives and educate us about our powerful history, only to be gunned down. All he wanted to do was something good for the community, yet he was killed anyway. After that murder, there was never another white man brave enough to serve ice cream in our neighborhood.

Eventually, everyone attracts what they focus upon. Bad karma caught up to Bee and Carlos. Bee was later shot in the head and left for dead, and Carlos got two life sentences in the federal prison. These sad stories are endless in the projects. Everyone has been touched by the death of a loved one or the perpetual cycle of intergenerational poverty and repeated trauma. Only on the other side of sobriety could I see how children could become the perpetrators of such violent crimes and how I became one of those young men capable of murder. The drug-induced changes in brain chemistry, the lack of structured education, a sense of righteous indignation, revenge, or the fear of being killed, these are the triggers that cause lives to be snuffed out before they begin. Be the perpetrator or become the victim. There's no mistake about it.

Chapter 9

BEHIND THE BARS

Five months after killing Tim, my sister Russhan neglected to return the car she'd rented back to the rental car company. She was late, so they reported the vehicle stolen. When the police followed her, she ran to hide at my grandmother's apartment in the projects. A nosey neighbor told the cops that my sister was indeed the girl who'd driven the car. The police couldn't locate my sister, but they insisted someone had to come with them. I was standing by the sidewalk, and since I was the closest, they grabbed me and put me in the backseat of the patrol car.

When I got to the juvenile detention center and gave them my full name, a warrant for murder popped up. And right then and there began my journey into the belly of the beast–the criminal justice system.

I never thought that I was wanted for the murder I'd committed. Since the police never came looking for me, I assumed it was all over. Although an initial flash of fear hit me, I wasn't too worried. I was only fifteen, and I knew I wouldn't receive a life sentence in prison. My mother reached out to Mike about the situation. Mike immediately got me the best lawyer he could, a sharp man named Don Winston.

A couple of days in the juvenile detention center weren't so bad, at least at first. My mother brought me comic books. My reading was still poor, and I could only read small words that I had memorized, but those books inspired me like no other books had before. The images told the story, and my brain tried to focus on every word because I actually *wanted* to read. I became the king of comic books during those first three-four months awaiting trial.

To pass the time, I pretended to be different biblical characters out of the Bible. Each night I entertained the troops and the other brothers in nearby cells. I guess we all needed something to occupy our minds. I was also trying to avoid thinking about all the money I was missing out on by not being free to sell dope out on the streets.

When my court date finally came, my grandmother and mother were there to support me, along with Mike and his parents. My lawyer worked hard to prevent the court from trying me as an adult. Mike and my sister's boyfriend threatened the witnesses that considered coming forward. To ensure his silence, Mike sent a few dudes to shoot some warning shots at Tim's cousin, who had witnessed the shooting.

That's how the game was played in the projects–murder followed by intimidation. If one member of the pack took a lick for murder, the rest of us ensured no witnesses showed up to testify in court. If a witness insisted on showing up, they feared a bullet would be put in their head before the court date ever arrived. Even the innocent community members of the projects knew this was how things were done. Everyone knew there were consequences to pay if a witness ever came forward to the police. At that time, I would have done exactly the same for any of my friends who needed help preventing a conviction. I was willing to live and die by that 'honor' code, and so were they. Snitches didn't just get stitches, they were killed.

No witnesses appeared at my trial. The court barely had a case without any witnesses or tangible physical evidence. However, they knew I hung out more in the streets than in school, and I had no solid alibi. There was enough evidence to sentence me to a year for manslaughter. Everyone was happy with the outcome of the sentence. I promised to have any of my friends' backs once I got out.

Initially, they sent me to a juvenile holding facility for delinquent kids heading to the Louisiana Training Institute (LTI) in Monroe or Scotland, two juvenile detention centers in the area. Once inside, I saw a few brothers from my neighborhood I hadn't seen for a while. Word got out fast that I was the one who killed Tim. Many of the inmates where I was headed were from the same project as Tim. Worse yet, one of Tim's friends had written a letter to a few guys in juvie explaining that Tim's killer was on his way.

I didn't know what to expect upon arriving at the holding center, just that Tim's cousins had a vendetta against me and that people would know who I was before I even got there. Things got real, real fast. During my initial trip to the infirmary hospital at the detention center, I was first handcuffed, as procedure dictated. Later, I sat on the curb in shackles while I waited to be treated for the beating I'd already suffered. Suddenly, I felt a boot kick my face. I didn't know what was going on. I heard a vindictive voice say, "That was for my cousin, Tim. You better watch your back in here."

A week later, I had to revisit the infirmary for a toothache. For me, each visit to the infirmary became a life-threatening risk. This time, I was hit again by another one of Tim's cousins. While I was handcuffed, waiting outside the infirmary, I yelled back at him, "If I ever see you on the streets, you're a dead man," and I meant it.

A guy named Blue offered to protect me from Tim's family members. I took this as an insult–as if I was some kind of a 'fake nigga' who couldn't hold his own and defend himself. As a thank you for his offer of protection, I promptly punched him in the face. The fight was cut short by the guards. They stripped us down to our underwear and placed us in the freezing isolation holding cell for twenty-four hours. This was the standard punishment for getting into trouble. I did push-ups and jumping jacks for three straight hours to keep my blood flowing and stay a little warmer. Sitting in the ice-cold tank, I felt so alone that night, far from all my loved ones, not remorseful, just lonely.

When my brothers from my hood found out what was happening on the inside, they wanted me to come to Scotland LTI so they could help protect me and fight Tim's cousins themselves. Everybody at Scotland LTI already knew I was Tim's killer, and the odds were stacked against me that I wouldn't be ambushed. Somebody, most likely me, would get killed if I were sent there. So, I requested to go to Monroe LTI instead, where I didn't know anyone.

There was some schooling offered on the inside but no appropriate reading interventions. The time I served in juvie could have been my chance to learn to read and realize a different path. I actually wanted to be able to read. I know if my learning difference had been caught early on, I definitely wouldn't have found myself on the streets long enough to get where I was. Instead, I was destined to maintain the same mentality about my circumstance. Rehabilitation was not on the menu. So, of course, I was destined to go back to the only future I knew.

I began lifting weights, which had become a great stress-reliever. I also wanted to get bigger and stronger to avoid being the weak one. I knew if I couldn't defend myself, I'd eventually get eaten alive.

When my mother visited, she brought me lots of goodies. Even though I loved those four visitation hours, I could also see the hurt in her eyes. Still, the drug life was all I wanted. Like many young black men behind bars, I couldn't see a better future for myself. Now, I had gotten caught, and I was part of the other dark side of selling drugs on the street–being locked up.

Every time Mike visited, he brought me heroin. The guests weren't searched and easily snuck in illegal substances. I could have sold it, but instead, I snorted it all myself. The escape made me feel better than I had in a long while. Being high again helped me temporarily forget the suffocation of inmate life. There's nothing like heroin to numb the reality of incarceration.

A month later, it was finally my turn. I was handcuffed and placed on the bus for a two-and-a-half-hour ride to Monroe. I had no idea what to expect. Everyone I'd talked to had told their own cautionary and taunting stories about this place. I was just fifteen and terrified of being alone. I wanted my mother, but I knew I had to show no signs of weakness. Because I was locked up for murder, I ended up in Unit One, the Red Bud, the absolute worst dorm I could be in. This dorm was known for a lot of violence. The fighting was constant, and the inmates weren't allowed any home visits. In Unit Two, inmates could at least go home during the holidays. In Unit Three, called the honor dorm, inmates were allowed monthly home visits. But here I was, stuck in the worst unit possible, with no relief in sight.

My counselor, Mrs. Thomas, was a young, white lady. I had a big crush on her. She'd let me make extra phone calls, so I thought I was special. I guess she was just being nice, but I naively and wishfully thought she was attracted to me.

On the inside, I got back into school because I wanted to learn how to read. I hadn't realized how far behind I actually was. One of my English teachers, an ex-nun, had a harsh attitude toward us. Most of the other guys thought she was the devil. Her authoritarian personality was a tough love kind of experience. Her approach was exactly what I needed.

I became the teacher's pet. She recognized how hard I was trying to learn, and she would give me extra work to take back to the dorm. She never called me 'dummy' and always referred to me as the kid who was 'trying.' Having this small affirmation from an adult gave me the drive for school I was missing. Her encouragement made me wish I had more of this kind of attention before going to jail. Where was this holy woman when I needed her, back in third grade?

As my vocabulary grew, I realized I spoke plenty of curse words and profanity. I never used words like: however, therefore, or moreover. These words were never used in my household or anywhere in the hood. I began 'sight-reading' books about cowboys and anything that really interested me. My method, or hack, was to write the words down over and over again to memorize each one by sight. In all honesty, I was still not able to read. As recent scientific evidence supports, this method of memorization is not how dyslexics or anyone with reading difficulties learns the code of how to sound out words with phonemic awareness. But, I could memorize the words, and I became more motivated to 'try.'

I knew that if I kept my nose clean, my good behavior would get me into Unit Two. I was eventually moved out of Red Bud to Unit Two, a much lower-key dorm with a better weight facility and a weight coach. I began to work out twice a day, and I built on a lot of muscle and developed a well-defined physique. I was eager to show off my swole during my first home visit.

The guard in Unit Two was a very 'out' homosexual. He had a big head of hair with a jerri curl. When he talked, he looked down over his glasses with an evil, wicked grin on his face. He was in charge of reporting the inmates' behavior and had sole control of approving or denying home visits. One write-up from him could cause us to miss the opportunity to visit home entirely. Like many in positions of power, he took advantage of his authority. This particular guard had a demonic spirit and capitalized on his access to young and vulnerable boys. Some brothers never got the chance to go home because he unfairly wrote them up and lied about them. I knew I had to play his game if I wanted to visit home.

I remember once, in the middle of the night, he summoned me to his office. Word around the dorms was that he liked to talk about freaky, even kinky stuff, to the boys in his care. That particular night, it was my turn. As I followed him to his office located in the middle of the dorm, I felt sick to my stomach. I despised what I thought might come next, and I feared whether my refusal would end my ability to visit my family. I had a sinking feeling that if I didn't go along with his advances, I wouldn't see my mom and grandmother. I sat down at the desk next to him as his eyes peered over me. He asked, "Son, when do you expect to go home?"

"I'm looking forward to going home for Christmas," I replied. He tried to make me comfortable by asking about my family. I told him all about my siblings, mother, and grandmother. I hoped that the more I talked, the less chance he'd have to talk about what was on his mind. He interrupted me in the middle of the conversation, "I have seen you coming out of the shower. How big is your penis?" I tried to laugh it off, but he was determined to continue this line of grooming talk. When he realized I was not interested, he didn't insist. "If you tell anyone about this, I'll make sure you never go home," he demanded. Then he told me to go back to bed. He moved on to potentially more receptive prey and woke another guy up.

Even though I never gave in to him, I noticed he often watched us in the shower. I thought to myself, I could kill a man like this so easily. In the end, he signed my papers to go home for the holidays and left me alone.

When I came home for Christmas, I was about twenty pounds heavier than the last time my family had seen me. I had fully come into my physical self. I had bulging muscles and a new, manly frame. My mother was overjoyed to see me home. We talked all night about getting back in school, how I could turn my life around, and make her proud. There was little response on my end. Even though she pressed me to tell her my plans, I didn't offer up much. For her, my sentence was a wake-up call, a chance to reset, and a stepping stone to a better future. My interpretation of my next moves was very different. I hadn't learned any lasting lessons. The streets were still calling me. Money and drugs were still my vision of a promising future.

The older people in the neighborhood welcomed me back to the community, hoping I had changed. I told them I had been going to school in jail and was a new person, but I knew deep down that was a lie. All my friends saw me as a force to reckon with and gave me a lot of respect. Because I was in jail for committing homicide, I was considered tough by other young guys ready to prove themselves, all the while searching for a way to earn more street 'cred.' Where I come from, going to prison for committing murder was equivalent to earning a college diploma. The people I looked up to most were proud of me. Instead of being admonished by my community and held to account for taking another person's life, I was rewarded. I finally felt like a real man on a pedestal, and I was still on top of the world.

My uncle gave me a welcome home party. I was amazed at how refreshing it was to be away from all the prison craziness, at least for a little while. Mike pulled me aside and told me that business was booming, and his cousin, Nap, was moving a lot of dope. The world on the outside had changed so much in the six months I had been gone. I couldn't wait to get out of juvie and reclaim my spot, to get right back in the game. My grandmother told me she was holding on to five thousand dollars for me. Little did she know I planned to use her gift as seed money to buy a quarter kilo of cocaine. I knew when I returned, I was going to need some capital.

I asked my grandmother about the money during the party. She informed me that my uncle had stolen it to feed his drug addiction. He'd thrown me the party in the hope I'd forgive him. Even though I was disappointed, I knew more money would appear when I got out.

Mike's mother cooked dinner and sat me down to discuss my future. I told her that dope dealing was all I knew. She told me she wanted me to do better in life. I couldn't tell her that night that her son was one of the reasons I couldn't give up the game. Just a year ago, at age fourteen, Mike was the first one who inspired me to put cocaine up my nose. He'd also helped to put a lot of money in my pocket. Our parents' advice to give up drugs and a solid income rang hollow. What else were we supposed to do?

Four days flew by, and before I knew it, I was back on the long bus ride to Monroe–back to the detention center–back to survival. There were so many uncontrolled thoughts rattling around in my mind. The small taste of freedom I'd enjoyed made me anxious for the next six months to go by as fast as possible. Especially at age fifteen, six months was a long time to wait for freedom.

Most of the guys who'd returned from their home visits had fighting in their sights. They had maintained good behavior only long enough to go home for the holidays, and now they had no incentive to behave. "Who cares," was our overall attitude. I only had six months left to go.

In my first week back, I picked a fight with an inmate who'd called me greedy. I was taken out of Unit Two and put back down into Unit One, where the other inmate's behavior got a lot rowdier. The next day at school, that same guy I'd hit, hit me from behind. Then, he tried to stab me with a fork. The guards grabbed him, and the teacher grabbed me. They called on the radio to send me to the infirmary for a check-up. While two guards talked to him about the incident, I walked up and punched the guy straight in the face. I didn't care about any consequences. I had been wronged, so retribution wasn't just necessary, it was essential.

I was sent to the 'hole' for three days. After isolation, I returned to Unit One, and I hated it. We could smell the liquor on the guard's breath as they beat us with sticks. It seemed they beat us for fun even when we'd done nothing wrong. Then, the inevitable write-ups would come, always stating we'd attacked them first. One night, out of the blue, the guards beat a boy with a stick in front of us. With each blow of the stick, he held back tears, but they kept on hitting him. After the beating, we found out he was shipped to the parish jail and charged with battery for attacking a guard. We all knew he hadn't attacked anyone.

The last months of my sentence passed by as slowly as you'd imagine. I was perpetually on the defense, and it was exhausting. I was in a constant state of vigilance, and fear became a persistent part of my life. I was always thinking about how to hurt someone badly enough to prevent them from coming at me. If someone crossed me, how could I make them regret it? Most of the violent incidents that occurred on the inside were usually stabbings. Shivs and shanks for stabbing people were easily snuck in or made from shaved-down items like plastic toothbrushes, strips of metal, or wood. Make-shift knives were less deadly than guns, but the threat of being stabbed effectively kept our threat detection systems on high alert.

Most common were the guys who were sent off to state prison to serve out added time for crimes they committed in juvie. They would graduate into another arm of the system, and most of them would never see the light of day. Their next sentence would always be waiting. After finishing their juvenile time, they were often kept in the system because they had hurt someone while still behind bars. The occurrence of recidivism was a vicious cycle. Once youngsters enter into the criminal justice system's hamster wheel, it's difficult to stop spinning from one criminal charge right into another. So much unprocessed rage under one roof leads to uncontrollable violence. The dangerous streets of the projects are much safer than what I found on the inside of four prison walls.

I didn't want to hurt somebody right before my release, but I was constantly provoked and fearful of being in the dorm. During my last week, I put myself into protective custody. I had seven days in the hole, and boy, they moved slowly. But it was worth it. I wasn't going to endanger my release date for anyone, no matter what I had to suffer.

When the shift changed during my last eighteen hours, a guard I had never seen before came in. He knew that I'd be released shortly. I asked him for the time. He opened the cell door and started slapping me repeatedly, trying to get me to hit him back. This was psychological warfare, but I wouldn't risk my future, especially so close to being released. I only had a few hours left of taking this abuse, and I wouldn't give anyone the satisfaction of keeping me locked up. I walked away and laid down until they called my name to roll out.

On Saturday, I was released from the detention center. I saw my brother, Dash, and his friend at the gate to pick me up. They were wearing new outfits that reeked of fresh cash. The drug game worked well for them, and I was eager to be right back in the mix. My first thoughts of freedom went like this: First, I could not wait to put on some fresh clothes. And second, I would get myself a new gold chain just as soon as I made my first score.

Dash had broken his neck while playing football. With his NFL dreams crushed, he decided to try his hand at selling drugs. Drug dealing was a choice for him to pursue. At the time, I felt like my brother was smarter than me. He seemed to have better self-control and a focused plan. In retrospect, I think of the ways we were different. My brother could read well, and he'd stayed in school. His sense of self was left intact. Perhaps we'd been raised similarly, but our experiences couldn't have been more different. Where he had excelled, I had faltered. Being 'smart' isn't the same as being able to demonstrate your intellect to others. I had been labeled incapable early on while he'd been expected to rise.

At this point in our adolescence, our paths had diverged far enough to be incredibly noticeable. His will to succeed hadn't been beaten out of him, and even though he chose to dip his toes into the deep end of the drug pool, he knew how to avoid the ultimate fate of drowning in disaster. He was doing what I was doing, but his approach and methodology weren't hung on the desperate need for approval and acceptance. This drug-riddled lifestyle was only temporary for him and very short-lived. Unlike my friends and me, Dash saved up his drug earnings. Instead of purchasing flashy items and wasting his money on material possessions to prove his worth, he got out of the drug trade as soon as he got the cash he needed to start a new life. He laid low and never spent any time in prison.

Chapter 10

THE WRONG PATH

I was so happy to be back in the projects. I was on familiar ground and in an environment that felt habitual. I was acquainted with the rules here, and I had my freedom back. My free will would compel me to jump right back out there, same dope, different day. My manslaughter sentence had taken a year of my life, but I was determined to re-establishing myself on the streets.

With murder under my belt and a year behind bars at such a young age, I became a bit of a celebrity once I hit the streets again. I quickly got back into the game. Several months after my release, a junky that bought heroin from me came back claiming there wasn't any in the bag. He was obviously out of money and just needed another fix. I pushed him away and threatened to bust him up if he tried to mess with me again. He proceeded to snitch to the police that I was selling. Twenty minutes later, sirens pulled up on me. Luckily, I had just sold my last bag and had no drugs left on me. Still, they slammed me against the car, went into my pockets, took all my cash, and planted three bags of cocaine and six marijuana joints on me. Even though I was guilty of selling heroin, I still felt innocent. They took me back to the station and charged me with possession. A week after my seventeenth birthday, I finally got my first 'adult' drug charge.

Even though I knew I'd been taken in on false charges, I felt the conviction was my karma. God had a way of warning me, but I still hadn't learned to listen. His guidance was like my mother and grandmother's advice–good to hear but impossible to listen to. For those trumped-up possession charges,

I was only given probation. Years later, those same two police officers who framed me, David Fisher and Larry Jones, were each sent to prison for almost a decade each for hiding behind their badges and planting drugs on others. There was corruption everywhere. From the top-down and the bottom-up, the streets were a difficult equation to change and perhaps impossible to solve without an all-out reckoning.

Just a few weeks after my first adult charge, my life started going downhill. Doe Doe, Dash, and I were shopping at Footlocker. I had about one thousand dollars in my pocket. Even so, I decided not to pay for the tennis shoes and strolled out of the store with them comfortably laced up on my feet. The security guard grabbed my arm and shoved me to the back of the store. He locked the door while he told the saleswoman to call the cops. There was no way I was going back to jail. I kept hollering through the door. Frustrated, I looked around for something heavy to break the window with. My eyes landed on the silver shoe sizer device used to measure the shoe sizes. With all my newfound jailhouse strength, I hurled it through the window. I thought this was going to facilitate a clever getaway, but the second I climbed through that window, the cops were standing there waiting for me to climb down.

I was arrested for felony theft and criminal damage and given a combined five-year probation for drug possession and petty theft. I now had three felony convictions and was considered a career criminal. I hadn't learned a damn thing.

My little brother Abdul was eight years old now, and my mother had a new baby named Ronald Harris. I felt terrible for causing my mother so much stress when she had my little brothers to worry about. My mother got me a temporary job painting houses. I got back in school, and things started working out well. My grades were getting better, and somehow, school became a priority for me again. I stayed clean for a while, went to class, and even did my homework. I think I was more motivated to face school because I enjoyed playing football on the school team. I needed a strong motivator to help me stay on track. At the time, football was it.

But this new focus was all short-lived. I was still surrounded by the bad influencers of the day–the same guys who'd brought me down even when I tried to make a better life–like some unavoidable lemming effect. I was surrounded by wounded people with habitually destructive coping skills. Drugs and poverty have always danced well together.

I met a girl named Cindy. She lived in the projects too. She was my first love, and I fell for her in a way I'd never fallen for anyone until then. I was seventeen, and she was twenty-four. We got an apartment together, and shortly after moving in, she turned me on to smoking crack. At that age, it only took one bad influence to trigger my worst habit. Before I knew it, I was trading in football plays for crack pipes. The old game I knew only too well how to play enticed me back once again.

One of my teachers at school was a drug user. I'd known him from the projects. I'd give him a daily supply in exchange for good grades and marked attendance. As the business grew, I'd bring half a kilo of cocaine to school for my boys to sell for me. This teacher would look the other way.

A flood of money started coming back in. By the end of the school year, I had forty thousand dollars in cash. Cindy and I took trips to Las Vegas to watch professional boxing matches. I was a high roller, and my life was looking just as I'd envisioned all those months trapped in lock up. I was getting what I had asked God for, what I'd prayed for. I thought He was blessing me.

My English teacher was a bright guy and believed in education. He always talked about how black people could do important things. He was very aware of my side activities. He talked to me about education and tried to be a positive influence. He told me that if I didn't stop selling, I would pay again and again for my choices. I thought he was full of it.

I accused him of being jealous of my brand new car, expensive clothes, and flashy Rolex watch–which were all better than his. I thought this man hated me. While he tried to tell me the truth and help me see the short-sightedness of my ways, I felt like he was only trying to stop me from achieving. He didn't have what I had, and he had no way of getting more than his teacher's salary could afford.

I was on the wrong path, and he tried to reach out. But I didn't realize that at the time. I was too far gone. I was a kid caught in a superficial trap of the marketing and allure of material possessions coupled with a complete lack of education. My status symbols were just that–a masked attempt at compensating for my own sense of inadequacy. I never questioned the actual value of the material possessions I thought were so important. My nice shoes and my shiny car were how I measured success. My poverty consciousness was all about the belief that I could never have enough of a good thing. I was not listening to anyone. My English teacher didn't understand my struggles in school, and no one recognized my learning differences for what they were. He tried to stop me from dealing drugs but never addressed the real root cause: my inability to read and my failure to meet basic grade-level skills. If a teenager or an adult can't read in present-day society, they definitely can't succeed–no matter what they do. The success stories of dyslexics who become successful entrepreneurs, start their own companies, or become millionaires with their "out of the box thinking," well, those people are the absolute exceptions to the rule. When the added social, economic, educational, and geographical inequities are factored into the equation, there's a thumb on the scale–one side is weighted down differently.

Chapter 11

ON THE RUN

It had been almost a decade since I had heard from my dad. He crossed my mind periodically, but I didn't think about him as much as I used to. I sometimes wondered about the people I'd come from and what my father was really like. I knew he had gotten out of jail and had no intention of seeing his kids. I had grown to accept that he was not a part of my world and that he'd probably never be part of my everyday life. When I was eighteen, my mother told me my paternal grandfather had died and that my dad might be coming to New Orleans to collect his inheritance.

My first reaction was pure joy. I knew the possibility of inheriting money would bring him back to New Orleans. Now that I was an adult, I wanted to meet him face to face and man to man. Even though he was coming back for the money and not to see me, I was still excited. After he made his plans for his trip, I heard my dad's voice again for the first time in many years. After we spoke on the phone, I got even more anxious about his arrival. He told me he'd be down in two weeks to get his hundred thousand dollars. I agreed to pick him up from the airport and let him crash with me while he visited. I couldn't wait to see him.

He said he'd share some of the inheritance with us, but I didn't care about the money. I had already made at least that much money selling drugs. I was just excited to see him. This time, he actually asked me about my life and how I was doing in school. I neglected to mention the drugs and instead told him I was a big football star.

The day finally came to pick up my dad from the airport. My sister Russhan didn't believe that he would actually show and had little interest in getting to know him. Dash and I were looking forward to his arrival. Dash was full of questions. I wanted to finally meet the man who I'd descended from. I wanted to see how he looked and how he walked. I was still desperate for a father figure and craved a version of manhood I could ascribe to.

Dash and I waited anxiously outside the Delta gate. Even though I had no memories of my father, I recognized him as soon as he walked out. I felt as if I had always known him. A broad smile lit up his face. We couldn't stop smiling as he embraced his sons for the first time in so many years.

As we hugged, I couldn't hold back my tears. The moment felt surreal. Since I was a little boy, I had been waiting for this feeling, this fatherly connection. Finally, after all these years, I was with the man who helped bring about my birth, my father. Seeing him in the flesh was almost more than I could bear. As we drew closer to my mother's house, the past pain, neglect, and lying flew out the window. I was so happy to be there with him. I couldn't wait to walk through the projects side by side so that everyone could see him. I wanted everybody to witness us arm and arm. I wanted them to know that he hadn't abandoned me. He had come back.

He was well-groomed, articulate, and looked a little like Dash. Sitting around the dinner table as a family made me feel content and complete. I wondered if I had grown up like this, having my whole family around, where would I be? I'd always heard he came from a good family, and I imagined that if I had been around his family's influence growing up, I would have been more focused on my education, and I might have made better choices.

I knew my dad was a drug dealer, too, so I wanted to show him how well I was doing and, hopefully, impress him. Dash brought him to the projects the next day to see my dad's old friends, and then he was able to see my whole drug operation. No one else I knew, who'd grown up in the projects, had their fathers around. I remember how special I felt all throughout that day, since my dad was there, I was seen differently. I could tell he respected my decision to sell drugs and wasn't going to try to change my mind. He understood. I was his legacy.

Later that day, my friend rolled a joint laced with crack, and we started smoking. My dad asked him for a hit. I was happy that we both liked to get high. I had wanted this dad and son bond my whole life.

My dad and I decided to go into business together, which turned out to be lucrative. With his new inheritance money and some old contacts in California, we reduced our costs by buying drugs in larger amounts and storing them in an empty apartment we used as a warehouse. Although I enjoyed our venture, we had differing business philosophies. He had a good heart, and we lost a lot of money when he fronted drugs to dealers he knew without checking with me first. After a few of his guys got away without paying us, I didn't want to continue working with him. He was too nice to the dealers and failed to instill enough fear in them or enforce any rules or consequences in regards to how we collected our money.

A few months later, I got busted for possession of a quarter kilo of cocaine. My sister was giving me a ride, and I had neglected to tell her that I was carrying drugs with me. She had no idea. Nine police cars were waiting for us when we crossed the bridge. When the police officers knew exactly how much cocaine I had in my possession before they searched me, I knew my friend had snitched on me.

I had hidden twenty thousand dollars at Cindy's mother's house. She told me that the police had found it and confiscated the cash along with more dope I'd stashed at our place. I realized she'd lied about the money being taken by the police when she bought a new car just two days after my bust.

I had to make a decision; either go to court and face sixty years or get on a plane with my dad and flee. We left together and took off to Los Angeles. After all these years, he was finally good for something after all. He helped get me out of New Orleans and possibly saved my life.

Even though I was on the run, I loved the West Coast. We moved into a nice condo. My dad had met a lady named Cecilia. Unfortunately, he said he wasn't ready to settle down with her, and their relationship didn't last long. Cecilia would have done anything for my dad, and I thought he was a fool to let her go.

Cecilia had a beautiful family, and I got close with them for a time. Her daughter reminded me of Janet Jackson, soft-spoken and lovely.

Cecilia's brother, Don, was a fast-talking, major drug dealer. He lived in a nice house, owned two Mercedes Benz, and wore tons of jewelry. Cecilia's mother, Mrs. Tanner, loved me like a grandson. She was a well-spoken lady with dignity and class who knew about world events and Christianity. I had never met a woman like her. She knew that I was an uneducated kid but completely looked past my ignorance. I loved hearing her talk about politics.

I had escaped New Orleans only to be introduced to bigger dope dealers in Los Angeles through Don. New Orleans dealers were like street hustlers compared to the guys I met on the West Coast. Even after all my encounters with the police back home, I still continued to sell dope. Many street dealers suspected I was a cop because my accent wasn't from their hood, but they still ended up doing business with me anyway.

I was still kept up with what was going on back home, but I had started a new life. I found out that a guy I knew from the Magnolia Projects, back in New Orleans, was trying to steal my brother's girl. He used to kiss my ass to get me to sell him cocaine. In my absence, he'd become a big-time dealer. I flew from Los Angeles to New Orleans and didn't even consider the consequences or likelihood of being caught. I was doing drugs again, and they made me feel invincible. I took his money with an empty promise of delivering keys of cocaine. I left with his cash, told him not to mess with my family ever again, and got back on the plane to Los Angeles. I later learned that he put a contract hit out on me. No one likes to have their money stolen, especially drug dealers.

I met some brothers my age who hung out and occasionally interviewed some pretty famous rappers. They had a company called Black Watch Production. We hit up all of the clubs and parties in Hollywood. This life was fun. I had started swimming in a whole different pool of contacts, and I liked the way this new western landscape was shaping up.

One of my first Hollywood parties was in Beverly Hills at the home of a former NFL running back named Jim Brown. This lifestyle was much different than the one I was accustomed to in New Orleans. I certainly never imagined that black people could live this way. I was definitely *not* in the projects anymore. When I first stepped into his house, I was in a trance. The entire back of the home was made out of glass. The patio led to a pool that hung off a cliff with a panoramic view of the city. I knew this was the life I desired. But my focus stayed on the most dangerous of paths to get there. I was ready to work hard for my money. My mind told me the quickest and best way to get where I wanted was to sell a lot more cocaine.

I continued to make cocaine deals and celebrated my newfound freedom with more celebrities out at clubs. I met Ice Cube and Eazy-E. I asked God many times why my life couldn't be more like these rappers' and actors' experiences. I would sometimes get deeply depressed at the thought of a life of insignificance. One night while club-hopping, I met Tupac Shakur. He spoke deeply and passionately on black issues. I asked myself what made this brother different from me. Although we both experienced gang warfare, Tupac's dreams were positive, while mine were colored with a lingering darkness I couldn't shake. Like so many of the brothers I grew up with, Tupac's story would catapult and disintegrate all too soon. During the height of his career, he survived being shot five times in 1994, only to be shot to death in 1996, at the age of twenty-five. There is no "Poetic Justice" in burning that bright just to get snuffed out because of a dispute over opposing disc tracks.

Other influences showed up in my life around the same time. Meeting Charles Dutton was a pivotal turning point in my life. I began to read about him, and his story captivated me. We shared the same narrative, and he had made it out of the projects. Here was a black man who'd served seven years in prison and had abandoned life on the streets. He knew about violence and broken dreams. He knew what I knew. A book of plays had inspired him to find his humanity while he served time. Why not me? I wanted to become an actor just like him. But the reality was inescapable. There was a warrant out for my arrest. I was still wanted by the law, and I was always looking over my shoulder.

After a year in Los Angeles, Dash and his family came to live with me. He later got an apartment right across the street. Dash encouraged me to take acting classes. This was a tall order, given that I was still living with a raging cocaine addiction. I finally got a job as a pipefitter. I learned the trade easily, and I didn't have to read to do good work. If I ever wanted to have a chance at memorizing scripts and actually auditioning for parts, I'd have to know how to read. I could see it, but I didn't know if I could 'be' it.

Cindy decided to move to Los Angeles to be with me. Her move diminished my depression, that was until we started smoking crack again. She would be paranoid all night, smoking so much. She always overslept and missed work. She somehow blamed me for her addiction and threatened to leave many times. Until one day, she finally called her sister to help her drive her stuff back to New Orleans.

I knew my life was better without Cindy, and I was able to admit everything in my life got better every time she left. At age twenty-two, I was finally ready for this addiction to be over. I met Veronica, a girl with braces and long hair. She was a genuine Christian girl who reminded me of my grandmother. She'd tell me about the love of God while we rode together in the car—she with her Bible in her hands—me trying not to use or blame God for what I'd experienced, who I'd become or where I'd been. She convinced me we should go to church together. I became somewhat involved in the church she attended every Sunday, but I wasn't ready to give my life over to the Lord. Money was still my master, not some white man on a cross. I had lost my faith in God many times. Yet, I wanted a savior to believe in, and I was conflicted with the desire to be sober and the harsh realities inherent in pushing dope.

When Cindy returned to Los Angeles a year later, my life spiraled out of control again. I underestimated the magnetic pull of drugs and this toxic love affair. I'm not even sure how I kept my job as a pipefitter through this period of my life. She upended any semblance of control I had not to use.

One night I asked God to lock me up if I smoked crack one more time. Be careful what you wish for. I was obviously so low that I willed myself to be locked up again just to escape my addiction. Faith restored. In no time, God seemed to come through and answer my desperate prayers. On the following Saturday night, Cindy and I got high. The following day, while watching TV, there was a knock at the door. I felt relieved when I opened the door and saw two police officers standing there. My addiction was so strong that I needed an outside force to get a hold of myself. These men were like God-sent angels on my doorstep. I knew something was already different. I had never been happy to see uniformed police officers in my entire life. I gladly surrendered.

They took me to the Los Angeles county jail lockup. It only took three days to be extradited to New Orleans. On my last night in jail, I had a crazy dream, perhaps a vision or visitation from God. There was a bright light over me. I believed God was looking over me that night. There was a sense of great peace, and I knew everything would be okay. That night, as if resurrected, I decided to break free from the chains of my past and become a new version of myself. My metamorphosis had begun. ~~I was thankful that my four years on the run had ended~~. I knew after this moment that there would be no more drugs in my life. I was done. They say most junkies need to hit rock bottom before the healing can begin. ~~I had reached my capacity for darkness. I was ready to reach for the light.~~

Chapter 12

PRISON CODE

I arrived at Orleans Parish Prison, a city jail with over a thousand prisoners, late at night. I knew this was a bad place. In fact, in 2013, Mother Jones magazine ranked this prison as one of the ten worst in the country. A million thoughts were rushing through my mind. My life had changed within a matter of minutes, the moment I stepped into that facility. As I walked through the intake, I knew this was my new life. They gave me one phone call, placed me in a jumpsuit, and walked me to the dorm that would become my home for the next nine months.

Life on the streets was all about control and respect. In prison, we gave up all power. The guards had complete control over our actions. They told us when to get up, when to use the bathroom, when to sleep, and when to talk. This was not living; this was captivity. This was punitive punishment.

After being gone for four years, it seemed as if my entire project was locked up here. I had seen so many familiar faces, and they were collectively doing *a lot* of time. The guys I grew up with who ended up behind bars were glad to see me there. Entry into their world was like joining a family reunion I never signed up for.

A guy named Put from my projects served food in my dorm, and he gave me extra food, blankets, and anything else I needed. He made jailhouse wine from the fruits he let ferment overnight during the week and served it to us on Fridays. We watched videos all night and talked about old times.

There were hard-core criminals on my tier. Inmates would come back from court with life or fifty or sixty years. They lived like dogs, fighting over phones and TV access just to keep their minds off their extended time. I didn't want to spend the rest of my life in this place. Luckily, I got along well with the three other guys in my cell. Jimmy was a rapist, and a jury gave him life; Hickey was in for stealing his mother's checks, and Tyrone was nabbed for a parole violation.

'Put' was serving life for bank robbery. His little brother was in for manslaughter, and his cousin faced a life sentence for murder. Put was a Muslim and prayed all the time. I learned about fasting from him. He'd go days without eating. I began to fast and pray as well. I apologized to God for all my mistakes and asked for his mercy. I didn't know if He heard or paid any attention to my pleas–since I had already done so much wrong in my short life–I didn't really believe I deserved his mercy.

Cindy initially promised to stand by my side, but just three months later, she told me that she was getting married. I was heartbroken. The toxicity of our relationship still had a hold of me even after we separated. I often couldn't eat or sleep. Deep into the long hours of the night, I cried myself to sleep in my bunk. At times I thought that I'd lose my mind. Cindy stopped answering my calls and writing me back. After several failed attempts, I stopped trying to reach out to her.

I was trapped in a living hell and needed God's word to strengthen me. Put coached me through these tough times. I cried to Put like a child crying to his mother. He was a strong Muslim man, and even though our faiths were different, he embraced me in my hardship. I knew that I had to leave the memories of Cindy behind. I was forced to sober up, on so many levels, all at once.

A new guy who was an older crackhead moved into my cell. He was a bright gentleman, knew the law, and was very familiar with the Bible. This old man saw my appetite for learning and my desire to better myself. He took me under his wing. I always thought he was placed in my path for a reason. He was my teacher in life, for when the student is ready, the teacher appears. I think I was the only one in that jail who attempted to learn from his teachings. The time I would spend in prison, this time around, was the beginning of my rise up and shine.

Sometimes, we talked all night and sipped coffee into the wee hours of the morning. He'd tell me that I could be somebody great because God had his hands on my life. I relinquished my fears about getting sixty years. God knew I wanted out of this cage. But if I had to do time, I'd love to spend time around this man.

Most inmates seemed to get a temporary reprieve, maybe even a sense of peace and happiness, from watching videos or from the new arrivals, fresh off the street, who'd bring the latest stories. I focused on God. My strength and peace only came from Him alone. Some mornings, when the rest of my cellmates went for breakfast, I stayed in my cell, stood on top of my Bible, and said, "God, I am standing on your Word to get me out of this place. I don't want to live the rest of my life among the dead." Put began checking on me frequently because the word had gotten around that I was losing my mind, which was mostly true. I was losing my old way of thinking and taking on a new way of being, adapting to a new mind.

Many in prison say they didn't commit the crime they were accused of, or the evidence was insufficient to keep them there. They had convinced themselves they'd be going home soon. I had committed the crime I was accused of. I knew I deserved the punishment I'd receive. I had no illusions.

I was a man facing sixty years, whose girlfriend just got married. So much pressure was building up inside me. I was a time bomb ticking to explode. I managed to stay out of trouble for a while until one day when my cellmate, Hickey, tried to take my spot in the phone line. As I reached for the phone, he tried to take it out of my hand. In a split second, I was intoxicated with anger and pent-up rage. I didn't tolerate being disrespected. This was not the code. Moments later, I lost control and became the villain I hated. The only thing I remember was his voice crying out, "I'm sorry! Please stop!"

After that incident, I didn't come out of my cell for two days. I realized that I wasn't mentally as strong as I thought I was. The old man shared in my grief as he comforted me. Emotional and intellectual ignorance was so prevalent within these prison walls that he probably found comfort in connecting with a person who was just as emotionally ignorant but was trying desperately to come out of the pattern we'd always known. He told me I must control my thoughts because thoughts become actions, and actions turn into a behavior.

I learned that people are incarcerated mentally well before entering a prison cell. The willingness to commit a crime in our minds fills us with self-imposed limitations. The outcome of a single moment of behavior leads directly to a prison cell. But the work of formulating a criminal mind takes years of training. He explained that by acting on thoughts of crime, we create behavior upon behavior until we are caught. If we could change our way of thinking for the better, our actions would automatically follow and improve. Impulse control was never demonstrated or modeled for me at home, in the streets, at school, and certainly not in the drug trade. We can only be what we see on our internal movie screens, but we can create a new feature film to star in.

On the brink of a breakdown, a light came on. I had to admit that my negative thinking was feeding my actions. As Buddha said, "What you think, you become. What you feel, you attract. What you imagine, you create."

We are influenced when we surround ourselves with high-minded people. We train and are trained by those around us. We synchronize our thoughts and actions with the company we keep, especially those we look up to. I realized the seeds planted in my young mind in the projects were those of poison ivy. I needed a salve to soothe my old wounds. Now, I had to decide where my future was heading. I had to stay focused on what I could manifest when I got out.

I often wondered, lying on my bunk, what a different life I could have lived if I'd just made different decisions and had different thoughts. What could I have done if I could have studied? If I could only read? All of these years I wasted, I could have studied to be a lawyer, a doctor, someone special who was making a difference in the world. I pictured myself as a citizen of my community who mattered, someone who could make a difference.

Anti-social values were destroying many lives along with mine. Black men were trying to build a life in the wrong system. The captivating drug world pulled us in and blinded us to the reality of a prison pipeline and which direction we were being pulled in. Each person in those cells became oblivious to the repercussions and risks of their actions. We became desensitized and risk-seeking. But this world was temporary. We had to wake up from these elusive dreams turned nightmares. We had to scream from the rooftops and call out into the streets, telling black men to turn away from this dead-end path. I would no longer be swept away by delusions of the streets.

The old man also prepared me for my trial date. He told me that most black men go to court with their heads down, never looking people in the eyes and speaking Ebonics. I made sure *not* to do that. I wanted to speak clearly and effectively–to represent how I truly felt about my past, present, and possible future.

A new inmate, a white art thief, came into my tier for stealing ten million dollars worth of fine art. His eyes were full of fear when he looked around, and I knew this white man had never seen the inside of prison walls.

He was tall, lean, and classy. From time to time, we spoke kind words to each other. He had a way with communicating and always got what he wanted because he spoke so eloquently. I still couldn't read, but I excelled at auditory learning. I began to memorize the words he used, and my vocabulary expanded. I began correcting myself when I spoke Ebonics. It didn't bother me a bit when black guys accused me of trying to be white. My goal was to communicate better and more clearly–not just to get what I wanted–but also to command greater respect. I realized that all my life, I'd spoken from a 'project' dictionary. I would now consider myself bilingual.

I found the African American history and literature Put shared intriguing. All my life, I thought black people were poor and destitute, but these books opened my eyes to a broader worldview. I wanted to read every book Put put in my hands. These were primarily pro-black materials I'd never seen before. My sense of self was growing with every story of black power I was exposed to.

Some people go to prison and begin to explore a wealth of knowledge. Guys finally get their GEDs or find themselves through faith-based religions. Unfortunately, once back on the streets, all of that knowledge may go straight down the drain. I decided I would make a conscious effort to retain and apply what I had learned. What if I accepted the fact that no one forced me to sell dope or shoot a gun; no one told me I was nothing, although I certainly made that assumption when my mother would say, "Now, sit your dumb-ass down." In the end, I chose to do what I did and did not do. I was the only one who could change me. I took responsibility.

When my brother came from Los Angeles to visit me, he brought The Autobiography of Malcolm X and The Greatest Salesman. Malcolm X's story changed my life. I wanted to emulate what he did while I was in prison.

I went through the dictionary, surrounded myself with educated men, and disciplined myself. While Malcolm X believed in Allah, I followed in Jesus' footsteps. Those footsteps could lead us to similar places. I wanted to rethink my ideals without the street's eye for an eye ethos beckoning me to participate in illegal or unethical behavior.

Jesus had taken hold of my mind, body, and soul. Put was a Muslim from the heart, and sometimes he'd get upset with me because I held Jesus so close to my own heart. My dad was a Muslim, and his letters were filled with his Islamic religious doctrine. Put was encouraged by my dad's writing and wished his dad was a Muslim and had named him 'Ameer Baraka.' I appreciated my name. However, my dad, who was also back in prison, never contributed positively to my life. So, in the end, I wasn't exactly elated by the name he gave me. Maybe I just hadn't grown into my name yet.

Word came down through the tier that Doe Doe had made the six o'clock news. He and six others had a standoff with the New Orleans police. Doe Doe and his crew were held up in the projects for hours because the officers were scared to enter their apartment. Luckily, no shots were fired, and they eventually came out with a white flag.

Doe Doe was already a career criminal facing twenty years to life in prison. Just two months before his arrest, when my sister asked him for money to pay for my lawyer, he got loud and told her not to ask for any money. This guy was supposed to have my back. We robbed together, sold dope together, everything that was bad, we did it together. Now he was right back here with me, and I wanted to confront him about not helping me when I needed him. We sent each other messages in jail, but I never had the opportunity to see him face to face while in Orleans Parish Prison.

I was sent to court on the probation violation charge, and I was facing five years for that conviction alone. The District Attorney (DA) said all sorts of bad things about me during the hearing. This man did not want me to go free. The judge asked me a string of questions about why I left New Orleans, knowing I was on probation.

I remembered the old man's advice I'd befriended in jail: Don't speak Ebonics with your head down in court and look people directly in the eye. I explained to the judge that I feared for my life because I believed the police would frame me again. I told the judge that I'd taken acting classes while I lived in California and was trying to do the right things.

The DA said I was performing on the stand. The judge had to decide whether he'd sentence me to five years for violating my probation. The judge returned after a four-hour deliberation and said, "Ameer Baraka Harris, I found today that you were acting in my courtroom, and son, I'm sorry to say that you didn't win any Academy Awards."

My face dropped. I knew that I had to do my five years. "I'm going to sentence you to eighteen months and give you credit for time served," he added. I had already been locked up for nine months. I only had nine more months left to serve for this probation violation. But, the other big charge was still pending, and I could still receive many, many more years. The thought of how many years I could actually remain behind bars was, at times, more than I could bear. My faith would be tested, and my fear was palpable.

I was moved off of Put's tier and relocated across the hall. The inmates in the new dorm knew I had killed a respected hustler and wanted to know who I was. The murder I'd committed was still following me. There was nowhere to hide. Still, I had to be vigilant and present a tough front because things in prison could go dangerously off the rails at any moment. My greatest fear was that somebody would try to kill me or do something to me to cause a reaction and that I would react in a way that would lead me to defend myself and cause harm. If I made the wrong move now, that miscalculation could result in me never going home.

During my second week in the new dorm, I needed to call my mother to ask whether she had found a lawyer for me. I got out of bed and started walking toward the phone. As I picked up the phone handle on the wall, a little, cocky guy came out of nowhere. He looked me up and down and said, "Nigga, that's my phone. You can't use it."

For a second, I stared blankly at the guy. I knew I'd have to fight him just to get my phone time. Nervousness and a surge of adrenaline came over me. Living on the edge all my life and constantly needing to gain respect and defend myself in the hood had always produced thoughts of hurting someone. Violent thoughts innately crossed my mind whenever

toxic
stress

I felt threatened. Having killed a man, I always feared hurting someone again because I knew exactly what I was capable of. This arrogant guy with something to prove was oblivious to what I could do to him. Immediate thoughts of beating him up filled my mind. I knew I could seriously hurt him with a single punch.

When I refused to give up the phone, I set the stage for a fight. In jail, it was second nature to fight and defend one's territory. I always lost all my reasoning when 'fight mode' took over my brain. I walked to get my tennis shoes from under my bunk and began to lace them up, mentally preparing for the inevitable. A long fight could start at any unexpected minute. Like a boxer getting ready for his championship game, I focused on lacing up for whatever came next.

At night, the guards were gone, and it was just forty men and me in a free for all. I guess we got lucky that night because just as I was about to throw the first punch, a brother walked up and told the other guy I was a known killer from the Calliope Projects. Hearing that changed his mind about fighting me. After that, I was able to use the phone without any trouble. Once again, that unspeakable murder I had committed almost a decade ago continued to get me respect. Unfortunately, that was the kind of behavior everyone admired. To other criminal minds, murder meant malice, and there was no 'fronting' or faking that.

In the new dorm, I met Solomon, who came from a good family and went to St. Augustine High School, a prominent Catholic college preparatory school in New Orleans. I liked him because he had so much potential; he could read and write and was incredibly intelligent. He also served in the Navy and studied dentistry, but he still wanted to be a dope dealer, despite his good background.

Solomon was crazy about making dope money. We knew the same people and used to have long talks at night—that was when he wasn't thinking about the drug game. I used to tell him about the harsh, non-glamorous reality of the streets. I tried to sway him in a positive direction because nothing good ever followed being a dealer. The killing and dying that came with the money would never justify the means. A part of him, deep down inside, wanted to get out and provide a better life for his two daughters. I watched helplessly as he was sucked into any conversations about the drug world—and

I could see how magnetized he was to the guys talking about their big game. There was a war between good and evil within this man, and unfortunately, evil ultimately won. Years later, he was still living the dope man's life, nicely dressed, with lots of cash, and he had all the attention of the girls, but still, as would happen with so many of the guys I grew up with, one night he ended up getting killed. A seemingly good drug deal gone bad happened all the time. No one was surprised.

In prison, my goal was to separate myself from all the negative social interactions. If I ever wanted to make a lasting change, I had to be intentional. Who I interacted with strongly impacted how I viewed my life and what I wanted to accomplish when I got out. I had to be mentally strong to fight off those demons and keep myself from being sucked in. How tempting and easy to go back to what was familiar and the worn path of least resistance.

Nikea Cash was one of the guys I enjoyed hanging out with. He was in for murdering his mother's boyfriend, who had continuously beaten her up. He got off with a lighter sentence–only five years for manslaughter. He had to serve just two and a half years before being released.

Cash was an educated brother. He came from a pretty good family, had a dad in his life, and education was important to his family. He helped me with reading and put me on the road to getting my GED. His dad always sent him books, and Cash and I talked all night about our lives. He always told me that I had a voice. With every positive voice I heard, I became that much more empowered to change. He encouraged me to use what I had, not focus on what I didn't. My parents didn't have to define me. My lack of a solid father figure was just a symptom of my street life. I was the cure. As I became more confident that I could learn, I became more determined to surround myself with people who saw education as a ticket out of recidivism, intergenerational trauma, and inherited social and emotional ignorance.

Chapter 13

FAITH

Time was moving along fast, and my mother still couldn't find a loan to get me a lawyer. I couldn't call my dad for help because he was still in prison for bringing kilos of cocaine over the Texas state line. I couldn't believe that he was crazy enough to jump into a car with all that coke. When I found out that he'd gotten a thirty-year sentence, I cried.

The judge who had my case was no joke. He told me that I needed a good lawyer. I pleaded with him to give me more time. I said a prayer and asked God to help Dash or my mother get the money. I needed some divine intervention, and somehow I needed a lawyer to represent me, and fast.

When Dash found out the seriousness of my charge, he was performing in stage plays and traveling around the country. One afternoon, his theater producer saw him sitting in a corner, crying, and asked him what was wrong. Dash told him about my situation and expressed his anxiety about how much time I might serve. The very next day, the producer mailed a three-thousand-five-hundred-dollar check to my mom to help pay for my legal fees.

As my faith deepened, God smiled on me. I got a great lawyer, Kevin Boshea. He was a little curly-headed, white, Jewish man with glasses. I could tell he was well-respected in the courtroom. We started preparing for my defense. He told me that the DA was very tough and had sent many other brothers to the Louisiana State Penitentiary for a long time, also known as the Angola Plantation.

Mr. Boshea tried to get me probation because he believed my life had changed. The DA wouldn't have it and offered ten years as a plea bargain. I thought ten years was too long of a sentence, and we turned it down.

After nine months of preparation, the courtroom was full of people on the day of my trial. I looked at the all-white jury and at each face of those who would decide my fate. I didn't feel innocent until proven guilty and was anxious and worried about how this trial would turn out. Would they see past my dark skin and intimidating demeanor? Would they pay attention to all the positive changes I had tried to make while incarcerated, or would they just write me off as another predictable statistic?

When young black men are faced with an all-white jury, they are often found guilty. I wondered what an average white juror saw when they looked at me. Did they only see the cover, or could they see the pages inside–pages that were illustrated with new ink. I was much more than outside appearances, a young black male with kinky hair, big lips, and dark skin. Would they judge me for what I looked like and the threatening appearance of a guy from a hard life in the projects? I thought it was safe to say they often just assumed that a black man was guilty without knowing much else about him.

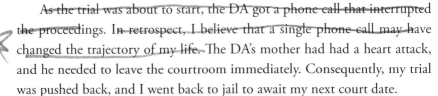

As the trial was about to start, the DA got a phone call that interrupted the proceedings. In retrospect, I believe that a single phone call may have changed the trajectory of my life. The DA's mother had had a heart attack, and he needed to leave the courtroom immediately. Consequently, my trial was pushed back, and I went back to jail to await my next court date.

God can work miracles for people who believe in the Holy Spirit and have faith in him to remove obstacles. I was determined to be one of those people. I read my Bible daily and became the leader of a prayer group. The other inmates always laughed at me when I sang church songs that my grandmother had sung to me when I was a little boy. I truly believed that God would intervene if I were sincere and pure-hearted. I prayed with all of my heart for the opportunity to start fresh. I promised never to sell dope again, and I meant it. If the good Lord could get me out of this jungle, I would be his humble servant. I swore that I'd make better choices if I had my freedom again. I knew I was changing, and I hoped God could see my commitment to a new way of being.

Months later, I was called back to court. Before the trial started, the DA called my mother, uncle, lawyer, and me into the judge's chamber to offer one last chance to take the ten-year plea bargain. He added that I'd get sixty years if I didn't take the deal. Again, for the last time, I turned down the plea bargain. I believed that God would save me as He had saved the prophets of old in the Bible.

With a new jury, one of mixed races, my trial began. Thirteen police officers testified against me. There was no question that I was guilty, but my defense was that I had changed my life and deserved a lesser sentence.

My lawyer knew that all my hours studying the dictionary, learning to articulate my words and speak properly would differentiate me from a gangster. By being poised, confident and showing them that I was concerned about my life, I took notes and presented myself as a clear communicator. I was no longer the same poor, uneducated black kid who'd committed the crime. The skills I learned in Los Angeles helped me carry myself properly. I took notes. I was communicative, and I premeditated every word. It was my life on the line. There was nothing more important than showing the jury that I was a new man and wanted to do better things in life.

My lawyer put me on the stand, asked me about my life as a kid in the projects, and questioned me about my time living in Los Angeles. He knew if he could let the jury understand my attempts at reforming myself, they might have mercy on me.

We had gone over the questions and answers countless times. I sat up straight, looked the jury in the eye, and spoke confidently. "My brother and I enrolled in acting classes to further our dreams of becoming actors. I worked as a pipefitter for four years to financially support myself while trying to become an actor." I added, "My faith is very important to me, and I have a strong connection with the church. While living in Los Angeles, I also became involved in local church youth groups."

The courtroom was silent as I spoke, and I could see hints of surprise on the jurors' faces as I clearly expressed myself. They probably expected something else–considering the serious nature of the crime I was being tried for. I even surprised myself when I broke through the stigma of being 'just another uneducated kid from the projects' who had made so many mistakes there was no room for any future. Showing them that I was hard working and had a vision for my life helped save me. The DA didn't expect that development either.

My lawyer turned to the jury and said, "Listen to how this young man speaks. Does he sound like someone who needs to be locked up for the next sixty years?"

I was sent to the dingy, musky cell below the courtroom as the jury deliberated for five hours before announcing my verdict. Twelve strangers were about to decide my fate for me, and the outcome was completely out of my control. I had goose-bumps from the chill in the air and the stress of an unknown future waiting for me. I paced back and forth, my mind going over my entire life. I thought about my childhood, the decisions that landed me here, and all my efforts to change.

The anticipation was the worst. I laid on the floor, crying for God to please have mercy on me. I said that repeatedly until I heard a voice in my spirit say, "Stand up. It is finished." I didn't know where this voice within me came from, but as soon as I stood up, the guard walked in to tell me that the jury was ready.

Walking down the long, dark, poorly-lit hallway, I felt as if I was heading toward a death sentence. Even though I felt like a dead man walking, there was also radical acceptance, mixed with a glimpse of hope and a thoughtful peace that washed over me with every step. In the courtroom, I glanced over at my mother, who had tears in her eyes. She was gripping my uncle for support. I could not read the jury's eyes, but I kept my faith. I was ready to hear whatever verdict they'd reached.

I can still feel the fear in my stomach when the judge read my verdict in his booming voice, "Ameer Baraka Harris is found guilty." The word 'GUILTY' rang in my head. That was the only word I focused on, and I didn't hear anything else. The finality of that one word was the most brutal hit I have ever felt. I was stunned into a complete state of shock. I had put all my faith in God, and I felt let down. Yet, the DA was infuriated. I looked up at my lawyer, who appeared to be happy. He patted me on the back, "Son, you are a lucky man."

I had no idea what he was talking about. I was just found guilty. How was that verdict at all lucky? He explained that the jury only found me guilty of 'simple possession,' which carried a two and a-half-year sentence. In New Orleans, however, the judge could double or triple the sentence for a multiple felony offender. My lawyer told me that I'd probably end up with a five-year sentence due to my four previous felony convictions.

My initial shock of the guilty verdict instantly transformed into gratefulness that I'd be able to live again. I was given a rare opportunity for a second chance in life and wouldn't rot in a prison cell for the next six decades. I couldn't believe that I had doubted my savior. He was my salvation. I knew God was looking out for me and had bestowed this miracle upon me. I had put my trust in God's brighter plans for my future, and my faith had won the day.

Back in the cellblock, the brothers were anxiously waiting to hear what they hoped was good news. After praying with me for months, they were excited and inspired to see that my faith in myself and my ability to work hard, with the help of my divine co-conspirator, had worked out. We all danced and laughed and celebrated this miraculous achievement. Miracles are real; I'm living proof of that. Who knows where I'd be today if that first jury was retained or if I'd taken the plea bargain.

I couldn't sleep that night. There was something inside me compelling me to praise my mighty creator. I believe to this day, God's spirit lives inside each and every person–if they choose to believe in Him. I say this with deep conviction because I felt something inside me that day I had no control over. I was at the brink of terror's edge before I heard the voice who told me to stand.

The next morning, I called home. My mother and I talked about how good God's power was. I realized as we spoke that I had been selfish my entire life. I had lived without concern for my mother, little brothers, and the whole family. I had never given much thought to how my mother felt about my drug dealings or how she'd feel if I had been killed. I never wanted to hurt her, and yet, I had. I promised my mother that I'd never, ever put her through this journey again and that I would do all I could to stay away from the life that had landed me back in prison. When I finally got out again and was a free man, nothing was worth disappointing her, myself, or my maker.

On the call, my mother told me she had something important to share that she couldn't say over the jail's phone. Two days later, my mother and uncle visited. She began by telling me that after my trial, she received a call from a lady she used to work with many years ago. My mother didn't recognize her on the jury because she was focused solely on me. My mom's former co-worker told her that many jurors were confident I was guilty. She had pleaded with the others on the jury to have mercy on me and convinced them to convict me of a lesser crime. She wanted to provide me with the opportunity of a second chance in life. This unbelievable story only served to strengthen my faith. I was a living testament to God's unconditional love.

Two weeks later, I saw the DA when I went back to court. He was determined to lock me behind bars. In the words of Jesus: "Do good to them who despitefully use you," and "Pray for your enemies." I was guided to ask the DA sincerely about his mother's well-being. I was genuine because I knew he must love his mother–just like I loved mine. He was shocked that I had shown this level of compassion for the same man who had been out to get me. He looked at me, and the anger in his eyes seemed to melt away as he softly said, "She's okay. Thank you for asking."

I was called before the judge for sentencing. He asked if I had anything to say. I explained all of the hardships I had faced growing up in the projects, being unable to read, and growing up in my most formative years without a father. I explained that when my father had come back, he'd led me straight back to a life of crime. I told him how I had changed, and for once in my life, I had a plan to live a positive existence moving forward. The judge looked at me sternly and replied, "Son, I grew up in the projects as well. It's not an excuse for committing a crime, and too often, black men use this as a crutch to continue a life of crime. Your poor decisions landed you here in my court, not the fact that you didn't grow up with a father. I hope you take this new opportunity and do something with your life. I am sentencing you not to five years but four years in the Department of Corrections."

At the time, I didn't fully agree with the judge's comments. I still believed that my environment and circumstances had controlled my actions in the past and that I had no other choice but to be a dope dealer and commit those crimes.

After reflection and many years of thought, I believe the environment I grew up in *did* impact my thinking, preventing me from making good choices. However, I had the power to take control of my actions and make my own choices. I was raised in a family that taught good Christian values such as love and forgiveness. I knew killing was wrong. I didn't truly believe or live those values because the power of money and respect seemed to be more worthy of my attention. Once I faced God and believed in the power of living a positive life, I realized that I could make better choices for myself. No matter what circumstance I encountered, I knew I could choose better and ultimately make the best choice every day, in every moment.

In the projects, few kids are taught ethical values growing up, and most of them aren't given an equitable education or non-punitive or positive discipline. Regardless of what children may be taught or what they face, young kids need to realize that they have the power to make better, safer, stronger, wiser decisions. We do not have to be controlled by our environment or culture. Our influences do not define us, and we can defy what no longer works to serve our highest good–the greater good. We can choose to live a life we haven't seen yet, a whole other life just waiting to be realized. Goodness can be taught and learned too.

Chapter 14

THE PEN

The year was 1993, and my trial was finally all over. I learned I would be moved from Orleans Parish Jail to Avoyelles Correctional Center, the Cottonport State Penitentiary. Guys usually wanted to stay in Orleans Parish jail to get frequent family visits and see their kids. But I wanted to experience the freedom of the penitentiary and get the opportunity to access their library and gym. I'd be able to work out and get my GED.

The Cottonport Penitentiary was located on acres of produce fields tended by the inmates. Brothers told me that everything, especially the food, was better there. They ate fresh fruits and vegetables grown in the surrounding fields. My youth fueled my excitement. I wanted to go somewhere new and unfamiliar.

Before my departure to Cottonport, I was placed in the brand new facility of Orleans Parish jail, a new dorm yet to be tainted and destroyed. This place had fresh beds in the cells, new televisions, clean toilets, better food, and most importantly, air conditioning.

The 'captain,' or the head guard in control of the new dorm, wanted to be feared. I respected the rules, but I wasn't intimidated by this guy. This obviously infuriated him. These guards were also known for badly beating the inmates and then accusing them of attacking first. If I had seen this man on the street, my old self wouldn't have hesitated to kill him. My new self still needed God's help in addressing my vile and sometimes violent temper.

One day, a fight started in my dorm, and the captain removed the communal television for a whole week. I got upset that everyone had to suffer for one inmate's stupid actions. I wrote a letter to the warden explaining that this punishment was unfair, and he gave our television back. The captain came back to work, furious at me for undermining his authority.

On Wednesday morning, around five o'clock, my cell door popped open. I was shackled like a slave; my ankles and hands were bound by a long chain. I could barely walk. The guards shoved us onto a crowded, hot bus. There were about thirty black men taking the ride to Cottonport. First, we all had to go through a screening process to determine our reading ability. All except one of us on the bus were dropouts. The rest read at or below a third-grade reading level; some were even almost completely illiterate. That day I realized that my struggles with violence and incarceration didn't just stem from exposure to poverty, lack of my parents' guidance, or the projects alone. What led me to this place was a complete lack of education. The main culprit of our doomed destiny was our collective illiteracy.

The captain was nothing compared to my arch-nemesis of illiteracy. A lack of appropriate access to this fundamental human right was robbing us of our future. Looking at the faces of the men seated in rows on that bus brought everything into focus. Education and the right to read were essential to breaking the school-to-prison pipeline. I saw each of us as a preventable statistic, and our numbers were horribly unacceptable.

According to the National Adult Literacy Survey, seventy percent of all incarcerated adults cannot read at a fourth-grade level, "meaning they lack the reading skills to navigate many everyday tasks or hold down anything but lower-paying jobs."

We came upon cornfields that I could see from afar, miles off the main road. The mid-June sun was up high. In the south, the sun shines brighter than anything. As we drove closer, I saw inmates carrying sticks with metal at the ends. Until then, I had never seen a shovel in my life. But soon, I became very familiar with how to use those tools.

Nothing in my experience could prepare me for the physical, emotional, and mental experience of the prison I was sent to. We were brought in to fill out our paperwork and be inspected. I felt an inkling of what it must have felt like to be a slave being sold at the market. They separated us by attitude. Those who had caused trouble in the parish headed straight to the cell blocks. My previous captain made sure I fell into that category. He had already sent a letter from Orleans Parish Jail to Cottonport Penitentiary about my supposed bad behavior.

Things started badly. Two white guards who spoke like they hated 'niggas' came to my cell and began to read the captain's letter. He had portrayed me as an untamed animal. One was chewing tobacco, and he spat into the cell and said, "Boy, you gonna comply here."

Imagine sitting in your small walk-in closet with bars on one door and nothing to read, nothing to write with, nothing to look at. I had a ten-minute shower to look forward to and only the hours to count down. After a week in that cell block, I was, "Yes, Sir-ing" and "No Sir-ing" just to get out of there, which took me about a month. Eventually, I was put in a dorm called Hope. How do you name a prison dorm "HOPE"? Hope for what?

I was often able to free my mind from the prison walls and daydream or time-travel to California for a few hours. But the harsh reality always woke me, and the realization of the remaining time I had to spend in there constantly interrupted my mind's fantasy.

Hope was a privileged dorm with more freedoms. Everybody wanted to be in the Hope Dorm because the inmates worked together, and the guards were friendlier. Mostly, older convicts, who wished to be away from the wild, young guys still fighting and stabbing each other, were housed here. The older prison population wanted to spend their time in peace. I began to understand the meaning of the word 'Hope.'

In Cottonport, every inmate had to do at least ninety days in the fields before they could earn the right to attend school. I never, in my entire life, experienced the sun the way I did in those fields. No trees, just miles of fields and blazing hot Louisiana sun. The guards examined our work after we completed each row. If our work didn't meet their expectations, we had to go back and redo the same row.

We worked in groups of two. I was a city boy and had no idea how to use farming tools. What does a dope dealer know about planting or picking vegetables? After a week, my partner couldn't carry my workload anymore and told me, "Brother, it's time for you to get this right." I got the message. I wanted to do better and felt responsible for pulling my weight. My work habits improved vastly. The more I did, the more muscle memory I developed, and the better I got. This was a habit of mind and a framework for what was to come.

Chapter 15

DIAGNOSED

An old guy in my cell block named Sam asked if I wanted to write a letter to my family. I tried to avoid his question because my spelling was so poor. I told him that I had to wait for store day to get paper and stamps. He went into his locker and got me a pad and a pen. After seeing I wrote like a second-grader, Sam talked to the guards about getting me into the GED program.

Everybody tried to get into school to avoid the blazing sun in the fields, but I truly wanted to be there for an education. I was ready to learn. When I was finally accepted, I worked part-time in the fields and spent the rest of the day in class. My passion for education became stronger. I planned to do well in school, so my teacher would recommend that I attend school full-time. I sat front and center every day and wanted to answer every question the teacher threw at us. I studied hard, separated myself from the foolishness that was going on in the compound, and focused on my school work.

When I was younger, I was embarrassed to give the wrong answer in class, but now I was serious about learning and didn't care what other people thought. At ages nine, eleven, or fourteen, I certainly wouldn't have had this mentality, but now, I was grown, and I knew the emotional risk was worth the potential reward.

After two months, I finally got into school full-time. There were twelve students in my class. Mr. Smith, my teacher, was a heavyset, white man who loved teaching. He made sure I turned in all of my homework assignments.

I remember one cold fall day, when I got to class, Mr. Smith had me step out into another room. Waiting for me was an older white lady with a beautiful smile. I'll never forget her. She seemed to have a love for education and for helping inmates who wanted to better themselves. Mr. Smith opened my records and asked about my upbringing and if my siblings struggled in school. I told them that my sister and brother did exceptionally well academically, but I could never learn to read—even though we all attended the same school and had the same teachers.

The nice lady asked if I ever saw my parents reading. I never had. She wondered if my mom or dad had problems with reading. Everyone talked about how smart my dad was. I wasn't sure about my mother, but I knew she could spell well enough to write all my tardy notes every time I was late for school. I told this kind woman I always made excuses for not getting up on time and avoided school because I didn't like to be there. I shared how not being able to read had made me feel dumb and made school hard, nearly impossible. I remembered my mother's brother couldn't read. But their family was so poor growing up that they didn't focus on education; his illiteracy wasn't a priority and had never been addressed.

The lady showed me all the letters in the alphabet and asked me about their sounds. I didn't have a clue about anything she asked me. Decoding words and blending sounds were so foreign to me. I only knew a few letters and wasn't able to read anything that was on the page. So I mostly guessed the answers she was after. If my letter recognition was challenged, sounding out words was like lifting heavy weights without any strength.

After twenty minutes, Mr. Smith asked if I had ever heard of the term dyslexia. I shrugged. In a calm voice, the lady said, "Ameer, I think you have a learning difference called dyslexia. Your reading scores indicate that your brain has difficulty reading, writing and spelling words and recognizing letter sounds."

My first thought was that her words confirmed what my mom had always said—I was stupid and dumb. Mr. Smith explained that this diagnosis meant I would have to work extra hard to learn to read and this had nothing to do with my intelligence. I told him that I wanted to be able to read and was willing to do anything to make it happen.

The lady who'd tested me walked me to the door, kindly whispered not to look down on myself, and advised me that I'd be fine. Finding the issue was step one. I had a thousand thoughts racing through my head. There was a reason I struggled with education, and it had nothing to do with my level of intelligence. Dyslexia made it hard for me to read.

I couldn't wait to tell my mother that I was dyslexic. So many people, millions of people besides just me, were affected by the same learning difference. Dyslexia usually ran in families and was passed down through genetics. I explained to my mom my inability to recognize letters and letter sounds. I told her the old-fashioned term for the condition was 'word blindness' and that it was harder for me to read because of the way my brain was wired. Dyslexia made learning letters and words more difficult.

At this point, I didn't know much about dyslexia and wasn't able to help her clear up the fog around this new diagnosis. My mom started crying and began apologizing for calling me dumb. All those years, my mother's harsh words, my grandmother's beatings for incorrect spelling, or the repetitive ways my family judged me, calling me stupid, caused so much internal shame and trauma. My mom asked for my forgiveness, and without hesitation, I granted it. A wave of redemption swept over me. My own displaced shame no longer swallowed me up. I turned my face toward the white cinder block walls, away from the view of the other guys standing behind me. I didn't want them to see the hot tears spilling down my cheeks. These were vindicated tears–the tears of recognition for all I'd suffered at the hands of people who couldn't see my hidden disability.

When I began to understand more about dyslexia, I felt a huge weight I'd carried ever since I could remember suddenly lifted. A relief greater than anything I'd known surfaced. There was an answer to the 'why.' All my life, I thought I was dumb, incapable of learning because I was somehow less intelligent than my siblings. But now I recognized that there was a reason I couldn't read, and it wasn't my fault. I thought about how many of the other guys in prison, the ones who asked for help reading a letter or spelling a word, were also probably suffering needlessly because of this undiagnosed disability.

A new chapter started in my life, and my days in prison became exciting. In order to rise to the challenge ahead, all I needed to hear was that there was still hope for me. To believe that I could still learn was the single greatest gift prison could ever bestow. I knew that I was going to learn differently this time, and my time in jail wouldn't be wasted. I began to put muscle on, but this time, it was neuro muscle memory, and the rewiring that was able to occur was in the synapses of my brain.

The following week, when I called home, I had to explain the term dyslexia to my siblings. My mother couldn't get the information right; she couldn't even pronounce the word 'dyslexia.' My grandmother got on the phone. She said she knew I wasn't just dumb or lazy, and that's why she stopped beating me. Thanks grandma. I had to forgive her too. She simply didn't know then the damage and harm she was causing. There was no amount of time I could have spent in front of that chalkboard that would have helped me learn to spell or read.

The inmates in the field were surprised that a guy with my reputation chose to go to school. The field had its advantages, like seeing the guys I hadn't in a while or getting the latest gossip. On the other hand, it was scorching hot, and I didn't learn any valuable skills out there in the blazing heat and unrelenting sun. I had no plans of becoming a farmer or getting involved with agriculture after leaving prison. I knew my future path was through the classroom, and my ultimate goal was to earn my GED. I had laser pointed focus. Nothing was going to stop me.

Many other inmates tried to escape the reality of prison by watching videos or movies. My time was too valuable for TV shows, but I made time to watch the news. My form of escapism was through books or by feeding my mind with educational material. Inmates knew I didn't want to waste time talking about street life. Reading was my new drug, and I always had a newspaper or a book under my arm. I guess in that way, I was like my dad. The old-timers admired me for having so much focus and determination for my future. I had been my worst enemy, but I could also be my own best friend.

My life was changing dramatically. My goal was to become as articulate as a college graduate. I decided to use the remainder of my sentence to gain the time I had lost in the classroom. All those years of repeating grades, all that time fighting to stay out of school. Now, all I wanted was a chance at proving what I could do with the *right* educational support.

Stuck on the inside, I surrounded myself with the most intelligent guys I could find. There were many knowledgeable black men imprisoned in Cottonport. They knew the law, black history, geometry, and other subjects and topics I wanted to know more about. These great minds, locked away in prison, never actually got to utilize their knowledge in the real world. As for myself, I was going to soak up all the information I could and use my newfound wisdom when I got out. I would be smarter and use that valuable knowledge to stay out of prison.

I knew I could never return to this place, the prison, ever again. Some days, after a hard day at work and school, I'd ponder all my old ways of thinking and the corrupted values that caused me to sit behind bars. I began to question how I could change the behaviors that might lead me to re-offend. What were the main mental patterns and habitual actions that led me back here? Access to education and my new beliefs and values would keep me out. I would see to that.

My lawyer had told me that the police had a tip that I was in Los Angeles. I connected the dots and figured out who the brother was that had tipped the cops off. That guy ended up in Cottonport and tried to convince me that he had nothing to do with my arrest. My deep-rooted Christian values told me this was a perfect opportunity to practice turning the other cheek. I now had the strength to forgive him. I realized he'd actually saved my life, not ruined it. For once, I wanted to thank him, not punch or punish him. If I hadn't gotten busted, I would never have stopped using. I would've sunk deeper and deeper into more serious drug addiction. I might have overdosed. I would've been swept up in violent behavior until the trouble finally ended my life.

Chapter 16

CAMP BEAUREGARD

After seven months in Cottonport, I was shipped to Camp Beauregard–a work-release camp in Shreveport, Louisiana. This prison was connected to an army base. The environment was the complete opposite of where I'd just come from. The inmates worked for the army to support the base, and the staff was friendly with us. We even had the freedom to leave the camp and go into town if our jobs permitted. These small freedoms made prison time more bearable. I even enjoyed being there.

Camp Beauregard held about three hundred inmates. These prisoners' attitudes were impeccable. There was probably only one fight every six months. The inmates enjoyed and respected the liberty they were given. We could go to school in the evenings. This place was a thousand times better than Cottonport. We were even allowed to stay up all night talking and watching television as long as we were on time for work the next morning.

Every day, I worked out on the iron pile and even had my own little office. The staff brought me homemade food. After work, I'd go back into my office and study the dictionary. I would intentionally leave my vocabulary words out in the open so others would know I was taking my schoolwork seriously.

I talked about my hopes for the future with the staff and guards, and they knew I wanted a better life. They'd say, "Ameer, as long as you do what you are supposed to do, we will do everything we can to help you. If you want something, just ask," but they warned me never to steal from them. Growing up, many of the black people I was surrounded with warned me that white people were no good. I've met some great white people in my life, and luckily, this place employed many of them.

An older black woman on the staff would take me into town and to her house. I liked getting off campus with her. She was kind and encouraging. However, I felt that she might have had deeper intentions or ulterior motives for taking me to her house. I didn't want to get involved with her. I knew any documented abuse of my privileges would reflect poorly on me, not her, and could get me into serious trouble.

My old friend Doe Doe was also transferred to Camp Beauregard. I was excited to see him after such a long time apart. My desire to confront him about not supporting me financially when I needed a lawyer had already vanished. Even though the new life I wanted was different from our shared past, we still managed to maintain a close bond as friends. However, it was clear we had become very different people over the years we'd been apart. Despite us both being locked up in prison, I wanted a better life. He intended to go back to the streets. With every conversation, I realized I was growing and changing in ways my old friends would no longer recognize.

Weekends were my favorite time in prison because it was our time to hang out, relax and chill. Doe Doe still had connections with the guys out in the projects and got updates on the recent killings that had occurred in the streets. Many of the brothers we knew growing up were already killed in shootouts or behind bars. Our hood was still just as violent and dangerous as when we roamed those streets ourselves. We felt lucky to be in prison, off the streets, and *not* dead.

Doe Doe, like many others, never took advantage of his time in jail. He was eager to continue the lifestyle that landed him in prison. He had no impetus to change. I needed positive influencers around me, but Doe Doe had been my best friend since I was a kid, and it was hard to turn away from an old friend. Besides those I knew in my religious groups or school, he was the only other person I chose to spend my leisure time with. Some of my Christian brothers nagged me because I spent more time with Doe Doe than I did with them in Bible study.

My mind was always on bettering myself–spiritually, physically, and mentally. I read a lot of different books about spirituality. Many of my fellow inmates, including Doe Doe, thought my faith was just of the jailhouse religion variety, and once I was released, I'd go right back to my old ways. I knew that what had taken place deep inside my soul, the voice I'd heard when I laid on the floor before sentencing, was my authentic self and would stay with me long after I was out of prison.

It was a Monday afternoon, and new arrivals streamed in. Squirt, who had introduced me to 'black mollies' (a drug just like speed) when I was only fourteen, stepped off the bus. I was none too pleased to see him. One day, I ran into him out in the compound and confronted him, "Why did you ever give me drugs as a kid?" Squirt looked at me blankly and said he hadn't known any better. I knew he was telling the truth.

I often thought about questioning every single guy who'd ever given me drugs when I was young and too naive to resist. What a cold-blooded thing to do–to give an impressionable young kid drugs for the first time and possibly kick start their journey on the road to addiction. I realized that drugs were such a way of life in the projects; no one thought better of it or calculated what an unfair start that was to a child. The innocent kids of the projects couldn't possibly know the potential threat inherent in getting high for the first time. I wished the adults in our community would have protected us, but we were all immersed in substance use and abuse.

Many of the social ills in the black community where Doe Doe, Squirt, and I grew up were a result of drugs. Buying, selling, transporting, and using only resulted in hardship and bloodshed. Hard drugs destroyed our community in so many ways–from children who used drugs before they knew any differently, to people who did desperate things just to get high, to men and women who were swallowed into some aspect of the drug game, to those who ended up as murderers. So many of us were complicit, and the problem was so rampant it was completely out of control. These were good people, but the power of drugs controlled their minds and changed how they acted. People inherited a predisposition to substance abuse from their parents or needed an escape from the harsh reality of our world. Without a formal education, many were desperate to make money or saw a quicker path to that ever-elusive brighter future through selling dope.

Yes, I had sold drugs. But I finally realized how powerful and lethal they were. I hated the part of myself that contributed to this pervasive problem in our society. I knew I could never participate in that world again. Being in prison woke me up to the effects of the drugs I had used and the destruction that followed. I never wanted to use or sell again.

Since the cops had found drugs on me and in my bloodstream when I was arrested, I was recommended to participate in drug rehabilitation groups. If I were ever to be considered for parole, I would have to face my old substance abuse. Doe Doe and I attended weekly meetings. We both aspired to make parole, and going to these meetings showed our effort and willingness to change. We needed the parole board to recognize we had the capacity to move past drug addiction all altogether.

I hated these meetings. I didn't necessarily believe what they were selling when they told us, "Once an addict, always an addict." I knew that I'd never touch dope and drugs again. Plus, I couldn't share my experiences with the group because everything we discussed became part of their record. I didn't want my past and addiction to follow me forward. At some point, Doe Doe told the drug counselor that we used to smoke crack together. I denied everything. I was scared my past would continue to define me.

When my drug counselor appeared at my parole hearing, he told the board I was dishonest about my addiction. I was furious at Doe Doe. Because of what he confided to the councilor, my parole was denied. I knew we were headed down very different paths, so I decided to keep away from my old friend moving forward. I wasn't going to risk any association or interference–from him or anyone else from my past. As far as my future was concerned, I was going to protect the opportunities I could and keep visioning a different horizon ahead.

Unfortunately, before my next parole hearing, I was sent back to Cottonport–for something I didn't do. An inmate in my dorm had an affair with the same woman who used to bring me into town and over to her house. Our phone conversations were subject to monitoring, and when the guards checked the records, they figured out there had been an inappropriate relationship. Since she and I had worked at the same office and she'd taken me out of the base in the past, they assumed that I was the one making the calls. The guards called me out of bed one night for questioning. I denied everything, but they were certain I was guilty. Even though I could've easily ratted the other guy out, I kept quiet and didn't point out the guy who was involved.

I took the punishment to avoid possibly getting hurt for being a snitch and was sent to solitary confinement until they transferred me back to Cottonport. When back at Cottonport, I was in lockdown for thirty days. These stents in solitary confinement taught me how to be alone. With time to think in seclusion, I could pray, think, mourn my old life, and even visualize a new one. Solitude became my friend. To this day, I can be by myself and never feel lonely. This adaptation has served me well. I don't need outside distractions to fill space or occupy my time. Although extended solitary could drive anyone crazy, I used these shorter stays to fortify myself.

At Camp Beauregard, I was allowed to get off the prison compound, listen to jazz music, and eat homemade burgers. Cottonport didn't provide any of that. The drastic change was frustrating, but I only had a short time left, and I wasn't going to waste my time being angry. I had to make this place work for me.

When my thirty days were up, I was sent back into Cottonport's general population. Many brothers were happy to have me back. So much had happened since I left, but I didn't care much for the gossip. I still enjoyed the conversations with the old-timers. They spoke about more worldly topics, so I separated myself from the negative people and kept gravitating toward those who reflected more wisdom than ignorance. I kept my head down–no distractions, no trouble.

I soon got back to my job in the kitchen. Shortly after, I started school. My GED was still a major priority. I worked hard and prayed that God would help me learn. Eventually, I got there. I was so proud of myself when I completed my GED. After receiving that certificate, my accomplishment only added to my drive to pay it forward. I even began teaching some of the GED classes.

During my last nine months of being incarcerated, my family often came to visit me. My mother was so proud of the dream car she'd recently bought for herself. Her face beamed as she talked about the car and the fun she had driving on the highway to come to see me. It was nice to see her lit up and having fun, even if it was on her joy ride to prison, to visit her son behind bars.

My mother had gained a lot of weight. I knew over these years of trials and tribulations, my actions had put her through a lot of stress. I promised her, full-heartedly, never to go back to prison again. When I looked over at my grandmother, I saw how time had borrowed from her looks and memory. She was aging, and her health was slowly deteriorating. She wasn't as focused as she was when I left home. She just kept saying, "God will see you through." I truly loved my grandmother. I realized that time was not infinite, and I decided not to waste any more of the days I had left.

There is something sacred about the last minute of a visitation. Every time my mother and grandmother walked out the door, their tears sliced my heart like a knife. My mother would always look back to check if I was crying. I felt like I had to be strong for them. I'd fight back the tears until I got back to my cell. When I was alone again, I let the waterworks go.

Those tears solidified that I was never going to return here. I planned to get out and continue to grow up as a full-fledged contributing member of society. Prison is like an island in the ocean. The only way to leave is in a coffin, transfer to another prison, or get a release date. Many prisons languish in these places for decades, and some die here, while others will leave as old men. I had decided never to return. This place would never be my Neverland. Soon, I would fly far, far away.

Let's go to Neverland and never come back till forever ends. -*Peter Pan*

Chapter 17

TASTE OF FREEDOM

Hopelessness ran wild in prison. Many prisoners were stuck in a loop. They could only talk about new methods to sell drugs without detection and dreamt of becoming big-time, 'successful' drug dealers. Others thought and plotted new ways to break into homes and steal more efficiently. I often pondered why, after suffering from incarceration, these guys could still consider jeopardizing their freedom—again and again? Being locked away in prison, working in the fields under the hot sun, and always being told what to do, certainly made me think about the consequences of crime and the cost of lost freedom. How could these prisoners even think about returning to a place like this?

I wanted to yell across the cell blocks at my fellow inmates, "Black men must realize that our wrongdoings hurt not only us but our families, children, friends, and all those we love. Your crime is pure selfishness! Let's find a different way to support our loved ones. Let's bust this damn prison pipeline into smithereens."

Systemic racism was a setup for wage gaps, poverty, and income disparity. Intergenerational trauma was ingrained and rampant. Mental health and safety weren't part of our conversations growing up, let alone learning disabilities or differences. Our school system had failed so many of us who sat behind bars. Budget cuts in education came from both the federal and state levels. Our government was not going to solve soon any of these issues—issues that have persisted and worsened with lax gun laws and gunmakers who profit while kids kill kids out in the streets. Our families are supposed to be the most important system of support. Absent fathers are not role models. In their place, examples of broken masculinity slide in and take over young men's impressionable minds. Our mothers, often single parents, are too busy trying to put food on the table to check to see if we're actually in class or who we're hanging out with. We don't end up doing what our mothers say; we end up imitating what we see out on the street. We do not grow up believing that we can become what we are capable of. We need to understand how valuable we are and that our potential is limitless. Everything is possible when we create the right circumstances and programs that support kids' growth and development as contributing members of our communities.

Incarceration changed my life. I felt like all the bad days in prison happened for a reason, and I knew I had a greater purpose waiting for me out in the world. I had never dreamt of becoming anything much greater or becoming a positive influence for the youth of the community until I spent those years in prison. Prison helped me dream, something that I couldn't do out on the streets. My dreams and goals kept me focused. As I walked the yard, I held on to my vision and always thought about the future. At night I'd stay up thinking about how I could earn money as a model and actor. I stayed in shape and focused on how my transition out of prison life could look. *"When there is no vision, the people perish"* was the scripture that kept my mind in the right place. I needed change to stick.

Every day, I saw how this place and the time I'd served had improved my life for the better. It was as if I had entered a reform university. I had taken full advantage of being sober and off the street. Before I came to prison, my vocabulary was minimal, and I was illiterate. Now, I could read, write, and even attend college if I chose to. I knew I'd make it in the free world.

My dreams of modeling and acting were at the forefront of my mind. My relationship with God was solid; this prison was where I had finally let God find me. He had gotten me through four tough years. When I first started my time, I never imagined that I would see this day. I was a new person in every way I needed to be. My resolve to stay clean and not to re-offend was steadfast.

I could almost smell freedom. Unfortunately, when I was this close to being on my way out of the door, I had to watch my back. One day, while working in the kitchen, an inmate pulled a knife on me. This man still had sixty years left in prison. He wasn't thinking about the consequences of his violence because he had nothing to lose.

Back in the day, in the projects, I would have fought him in order not to look weak. But now, so close to my release, I decided not to respond to being provoked. I backed down and walked away. I valued my family, dreams, and the freedom that existed on the other side of these walls. More than others' opinions about me, what mattered most was my ability to release myself from the grip of the penal system.

In my last few days at work, they gave me the hardest chores in the kitchen. The sergeant made me unload all the big trucks. With each heavy box I moved, I vowed never to commit another crime. Even though they worked me all day, I felt like I was walking on air. The other kitchen workers laughed at me. I knew their laughter was in vain because I was leaving, and they were not. I thought, "I'm never coming back here again. I will never see these people again."

My last twenty-four hours in prison are permanently etched in my brain. My sister told me on the phone that she'd pick me up at Cottonport. The guys in the dorm came to say their goodbyes. I got my hair trimmed that night, and my excitement kept me from sleeping. To leave that next morning was almost too good to be true.

I laid in my bunk thinking about all the things I wouldn't have to do. No more waking up early, being told what to do and where to do it. No more picking vegetables in the hot sun or serving food to other inmates. No line for the phone or feeling the desperation of being cut off from truly living. I wanted a full life, and I was ready to lead myself in the direction I'd had four years to plot. My life could start now.

The next day, I heard the guards call my name to leave. I quickly got my few belongings together. I walked out of the dorm and never looked back. Walking down the long hallway to the exit felt never-ending. I was finally leaving this place. As I approached the exit door, a guard's voice came through the microphone, telling me he'd see me again soon. I just shrugged at him and laughed. I knew he was wrong. He couldn't see my resolve, and he couldn't feel what I was feeling at the prospect of being free. I knew that I'd never step inside these prison walls again. The horrible things I had seen and been through were all over now. Prison and serving time had been a trauma in and of itself. And paradoxically, the prison had also saved my life.

Chapter 18

THE UNSPEAKABLE

After walking out the prison doors, I was placed in the prison truck and rolled up toward the front gate. To my great relief, my sister was waiting for me. When the last gate opened, I felt the peace that only another inmate could understand. Though it was dark, I felt like the sun shone on my face. To be outside of the walls of the prison was to feel truly alive. To smell the fresh air of freedom smelled sweeter than sweet. The level of my joy was beyond any words.

As I got out of the truck, a free man, I kissed the ground and thanked the Lord. Then I ran to my sister. She refused to visit me in jail, and we hadn't seen each other in four years. We had so much to catch up on.

I received an eighty-dollar check for four years of my work in prison. Our first stop was a small gas station store still open after midnight to get a snack. I gave a dollar to the beautiful girl behind the counter for a Snickers bar. I kept talking to her while my sister was shopping. How fun it was to interact with a woman again.

In the car, my sister turned on the latest rap songs. "This is P from our neighborhood!" she exclaimed. Master P's music was off the chain. I bobbed my head to the beat and listened intently to his lyrics.

During the two-and-a-half-hour drive to New Orleans that night, my sister filled me in on what I had missed over the years. She told me her kids were excited to see me. I hadn't seen them since they were very young. We talked about my friends in the neighborhood. My sister warned me about another threat spreading on the streets–AIDS. Eventually, my sister was tired of driving, and I was tired of listening to her chatter about the gossip I'd missed. I took the wheel to allow her to nap. I had no license. Committing even a minor infraction made me feel sick to my stomach.

When my mother opened the door and saw me, she had tears of happiness running down her face. I held her close and tight in my arms as she cried. She knew I loved fried trout, and even though it was about four o'clock in the morning, she had my favorite dish waiting for me. It was such a joy to be home with my family. I was relieved beyond measure.

Including the four years on the run, I had been away from home for eight years. My grandmother walked out slowly from the back room, struggling with her old age. Her mobility had slowed her down even more. She looked up and said, "Lord, thank you for bringing my grandson home." We all held hands, and my grandmother praised God.

Everything in my mother's house looked smaller than I remembered. The doors, hallways, and even the bedrooms were small. I knew I had an obligation to my younger self to make something of my life now that I was older and had lived to see my family once more. I wanted to get my family out of this tiny house. I realized that my motivation for things in life had not really changed that drastically. Whether through proceeds from drugs or acting, I always wanted to care for my mother and the entire family. I had put them through so much pain and strife, never realizing that my mom never really wanted me to give her money, gifts, or a bigger house. She just wanted a better life for me than the one I'd been living.

The following day, I visited several of my old friends in the projects. Nothing seemed to have changed. Everyone was doing the exact same things on the streets as eight years ago. Brothers were just hanging out, drinking beer, and talking the same trash talk I remembered. Some of the guys, who thought I'd pick up where I left off, weren't as excited to see me. I had no intention of reclaiming my territory. I was determined to follow my dreams of becoming an actor, and I was determined to make them real.

My day was going well until I came home to find Russhan and my mother in a hot argument. My sister had never acted this way before, and I had never seen her cry with such heartache. Growing up, I didn't understand why Russhan never showed any love or affection towards my mother. That day it all became apparent. Sobbing, she recounted the horrors that Steve, one of my mother's boyfriends, inflicted upon her. He was the one who said he wanted a daughter and always had Russhan sit on his lap. She told us how it all started. "Mama had left for work, and Steve watched me until Grandma picked me up after she got off work. Steve led me into Mama's room one afternoon and told me to lay there quietly."

Dash and I sat there, shocked and stunned, as we were clueless about how any of this had occurred without us knowing. It was difficult to hear where this story was heading. This was my sister, and the thought of someone sexually assaulting her rekindled my desire to kill again.

"Steve laid me down on the bed, lifted my shirt, and began to rub and kiss my breasts," she continued. Hearing her recollect this abuse made me nauseous, and with each tear rolling down her cheek, my rage became uncontrollable and inextinguishable.

"He unzipped my pants and rubbed on my private area," she added. "Milly, I was so scared. Mama was gone, and I didn't know what to do. I finally told her about this assault, but she never did anything."

My mother's eyes filled with tears. I wondered how she could have let this happen. How could she have brought this predator into our home? Steve had managed to feed off the most innocent in our family. I blamed her weakness and tendency to always having a man around. She had brought a snake into our lives who had repeatedly preyed on my sister.

My sister's trauma of abuse held a cascade of regret. My sister blamed our mother for never being there for her when she wanted her love. I realized that Russhan still felt the same void I felt about my dad's absence. Even though my mother was around, she had missed a lot and failed to protect us from the potential of being young and vulnerable to predators.

Russhan said she was never the same after repeatedly being molested by Steve. To her, this was my mother's ultimate betrayal. At some point, my sister confided in my grandmother because afterward, my grandmother never allowed my sister to revisit my mother's house. During the rest of our childhood, I had no idea why my brother and sister and I lived in separate places.

After hearing my sister's story, I was never the same either. How could a grown man rob a child of their dignity and innocence? Dash and I sat there, filled with shock and anger. We both wanted this monster to feel our wrath and get revenge, but Dash was not the violent type.

"Where does Steve live now?" I demanded with my sights set on payback. "I will find him, and I *will* kill him." As I continued shouting, I cursed in front of my mother for the first time. I questioned my mother about why she didn't tell us or protect our sister. How could our family hide this secret for so long? She just sat there in silence, knowing she had been ignorant for not seeing what Steve was capable of. She could see now how much pain this misjudgment of character had caused our family.

To this day, my sister still hates our parents. Before it all came out, I never understood my sister's harsh resentment and harbored anger against them. My mother trusted this predator to be unsupervised around my sister, never thinking of the risk to her daughter's welfare. My mother had wanted a man around, not realizing or suspecting that he could be molesting her daughter. For my dad's part, he wasn't there at all and chose to chase drugs and money over the responsibility he had to support us–physically, emotionally, and financially.

As my sister shared her story, a flood of memories flooded back to me. My own suppressed childhood secrets began to unravel. I was about six or seven, and my grandmother let me spend the night at my aunt's house. My cousin and I had dinner and watched TV as my grandmother and aunt left to hang out in the other room. I think my cousin was around fourteen at the time, but he appeared much older than my brother and me. That night we slept on the sofa bed in the living room. There was a good cowboy movie playing in the background.

I was exhausted and must have fallen into a deep sleep. I woke up to a startling shock. Suddenly, I felt a hand in my underwear. A fear that I had never experienced before paralyzed me. I just wanted my cousin to stop but couldn't find the words or actions to end or question what he was doing. I have no idea how long he played in my underwear, but it felt like hours. I couldn't go back to sleep that night. I laid there frozen with horror as tears rolled down my face in the dark.

The next morning, I got up and hoped to forget everything that had happened. I never wanted to think about the incident ever again. I decided I'd never go back to my cousin's house to play. I never told anyone what had happened. Just like Russhan, the inappropriate sexual contact was a secret that I was ashamed of.

My cousins grew up mentally unstable. One became an alcoholic, and the other had severe anger problems. I hadn't ever understood why they were such a hot mess after coming from what looked like a stable home. Maybe something traumatic happened to them as well. Perhaps my cousin was only emulating abuse he himself had suffered. As an adult, my cousin stayed away from the family. I believe he may have made the same sort of sexual advances to all of us who had spent the night there. He may have feared the truth would come out eventually. Last I heard, he was dying of AIDS in San Francisco. Family secrets only allowed abuse to be passed down from generation to generation. A code of silence perpetuated more abuse.

Even though I never wanted to think about that night after it happened, and I locked the incident out of my mind, it was time to share this memory with my mother. What my cousin had done was wrong. Sadly, considering what I had heard other children were forced to do, I actually felt blessed that I wasn't coerced into participating in other more nefarious sexual activities. What a twisted world to live in. How many children had to navigate these circumstances long before they were emotionally prepared to handle them?

My mother broke down and told me her uncle used to touch her when she was a little girl. My mother overheard his wife, a church-going lady, confront this man when she learned he molested his own grandkids. My mother was a dark-skinned, black girl who didn't feel like she had a voice. She carried a sense of shame that made her a perfect target for an abuser. He capitalized on her insecurities and counted on her silence. This type of abuse only added to my and my sibling's emotional baggage. Sexual abuse can have severe psychological effects on children, manifesting different struggles long into adulthood. Molesters can paralyze their child victims, threatening them or silencing them in the sea of shame their sexual exploitation creates. My mother, Russhan, and I had experienced trauma that could have ruined our lives. We were each victimized by someone we trusted. And for years, we chose not to say a thing about it to one another.

My mother was still a kid when she had three babies–Russhan, Dash, and I. As a young mother, she was absent in our formative years–both physically and emotionally. While she was running around out in the projects playing street games and hanging out with her friends, my grandmother stepped in and raised us in the best and only way she knew. Her infamous beatings were authoritarian, but the fear of pain she wielded, like so many other parents of that mindset, was intended to inspire and encourage us to do well in school and stay out of trouble.

Although my mother was what I now consider to be a delinquent mother, I always knew she loved us with all her heart and wanted the best for us. As I chased my dreams and was ready to give up, she always believed in me and encouraged me to stay in the fight and keep aspiring to reach higher.

And I've forgiven her for all she had and hadn't done. I proudly walked down the red carpet with her in 2019 at my Emmy nomination. I was happy to have her beside me, to have her on my arm.

My father, on the other hand, I've never been able to forgive full-heartedly. All these years, he had been selfish and remained 'father' in name only. Men can serve as sperm donors, *or* they can stand by their children through all the hurts and triumphs and send their kin out into the world armed with the best possible start in life. Like so many black fathers, my dad was the former. Maybe there's still a chance for forgiveness there. I still aspire to grant him enough grace for a relationship between us to exist.

Chapter 19

BLIND FAITH

After only seven days of being back home, I just had to leave New Orleans, so I flew back to Los Angeles. My mother begged me to stay longer and spend time with her, but I couldn't. A week in my old house, on those old streets, was all I could handle.

I was twenty-seven years old and finally a free man out to pursue his dreams. For once in my life, I had a laser-pointed vision for my future. My heart was on fire with the goals and dreams I'd been saving up for freedom's gate. I was ready for the gate to be flung wide open and saunter through. I didn't care how many people were ready to support my vision of a new life. Any roadblock to success, any person who thought to challenge my every step, they best get out of the way because I was here to do good things. I was determined to surround myself with positive people who had their own visions; individuals who would support me and motivate me to get to where I was going.

My brother, Dash, was still in Los Angeles with his family. I moved in with them for a short while. I soon found a job again as a pipefitter with an old friend, Earl. They started me out at fifteen dollars an hour, which was good money at the time. Life was moving along well. I was making an honest living and saving for my dreams. Every evening, when I looked at my dirty reflection in the mirror, I reminded myself that this was only temporary. I got my modeling portfolio set up. It was time for me to stand up on my own two feet.

Month after month, modeling agencies turned me down, saying they had somebody who looked exactly like me. I was discouraged and began to doubt my decision to pursue acting as a career. I had to gain peace again as I was starting to lose hope. I asked God to help guide me.

A voice inside my head told me to go back to the LA Model Agency I'd visited the week prior. To my surprise, this time, they signed me on. This was a big step. My mother was excited and proud of me. For once, her son was finally doing something positive.

I began getting jobs through LA Models. Things were looking up, that was until I gave my number directly to a company that wanted me to model their clothes. My agent was mad when he found out about it. "I told you never to give your phone number to a client. I don't care if it's your mother who asked for your personal number," he yelled. I naively told him that my mother had nothing to do with this, and minutes later, I was released from the agency. Apparently, models aren't supposed to talk back to their agents.

I felt my world had come apart. It took me a while to find a new agent. In the meantime, I continued to work as a pipefitter. Some nights I cried because my life seemed useless. I had read many books and contemplated these moves for four years. I had always heard that all I had to do was work hard and believe. I thought I'd achieve what I wanted if I went after it. I didn't realize how difficult going after my goal would actually *be*. To have irreversible blind faith in my life's purpose and the effort involved in never, ever giving up on myself was going to be more difficult than I'd thought.

I had considered going back to school when I got out of prison. I contemplated playing it safer. I had the opportunity to get into physical therapy school back in New Orleans. But the entertainment business was like a new version of cocaine to my addict brain, and I had already gotten my first hit. There was no turning back on my first real dream and goal in life. I didn't want to give this acting vision up so easily. Even after the pain and tears, somehow, I mustered up the strength and courage to continue in Los Angeles.

I quit my job as a pipefitter and went into modeling full-time–which meant an unstable income and inconsistent money-making potential. I befriended a few girls who worked in restaurants, and they fed me.

My mother called and somehow knew that my situation had become deplorable. She'd promptly send me thirty or forty dollars for food, just enough to get me by.

Shortly after passing up the chance to go to physical therapy school, I crossed paths at the Hilton Hotel with a familiar face from my old neighborhood. It was Master P.

Master P was on his way out when we ran into each other. We talked for a couple of minutes. He gave me his number just before his security team rushed him off. He had made it big and was now a famous rap mogul, while I was a man who was going under while waiting for any door to open wide enough to squeeze through. He could probably see the desperation and determination all over my face. We had recognizable roots—we both knew where the other had come from—and how far I'd have to reach and stretch to touch a different life.

After making several fruitless attempts to reach him, I realized that he was probably too busy for me. However, I couldn't let this opportunity slip away. He was my brother from the Calliope projects, and I needed his help.

I had heard that Master P was in Atlanta at the NBA tryouts for the Charlotte Bobcats. I took my rent money and used it to buy a flight to Atlanta. On blind faith, without a second thought, I trusted my gut and went after the remote possibility that I could connect with him again. This was the last little bit of money I had to my name, and I was either going to get a job with Master P or get kicked out of my apartment. I thought it was worth the gamble.

With sixty-three dollars left in my pocket, I checked into a cheap hotel room for the night. I searched, without luck, to find a ticket I could afford so that I could attend the tryouts. When a food delivery boy went in through the stadium's back door, and it didn't fully shut, I took a major chance and desperately put my freedom back on the line. I grabbed the door and slipped in. I took the elevator to the arena. This was a big gamble with my freedom. Even a minor infraction could send me packing back to a life I'd sworn never to live again.

Once I was in the arena, it was easy to spot Master P. He was surrounded by about twenty guys in camouflage shirts with lots of jewelry on. I knew a few brothers, and they invited me into their circle. After the game, I met up with Master P. We talked about what I wanted out of life. He mentioned that he was about to come out with a clothing line soon. He took my cell phone number and address.

After telling him about my situation and how I got there, he put me up in a hotel for the night and paid for my food. Master P treated me well. The hotel room he splurged for was not in just any hotel; it was at the Ritz-Carlton, where he was also staying. The bed was plush, the food was free, and I was hungry. I had filet mignon, mashed potatoes, and a glass of Pinot Noir for dinner. That night I watched Sidney Poitier's Raisin in the Sun. As I sat enjoying my steak, I was inspired by Poitier's acting abilities. The next morning, I ordered everything I could eat for breakfast. I stayed as long as I could in that hotel and didn't leave until the very last minute. Another taste–just enough of a sample of comfort and plenty to keep me wanting more. I knew I wanted to try to spend the rest of my life in places just like this one, not in some dingy motel in desperation and obscurity.

When I got back to Los Angeles, there was already a FedEx package with a ten-thousand-dollar check from Master P waiting in my mailbox. He wanted to help me out until we could meet up again. I couldn't believe his generosity. He knew what a pivotal and perilous place I was really in. I had used the rent money for the Atlanta trip, and I would have been on my way back to the streets if it wasn't for his check. I held the paper in my hands and just stared. God was looking out for me. This was just one more proof.

I had lived frugally in my Los Angeles apartment. I made every penny count because I had to. I had nothing but a bed, an old television, and a few kitchen tools. Soon after the check arrived, I moved to Baton Rouge, Louisiana, where Master P's record label, No Limit Records, was located. I left everything behind in that tiny apartment and got on a plane back down south with only a single carry-on bag.

A well-furnished and plush apartment–with a year's rent paid upfront by Master P–was waiting for me in Baton Rouge. He eventually signed me for a sixty-thousand-dollar modeling deal for his clothing line. I traveled with him during concerts and the good times turned great. People loved him and his two brothers. All three of them had managed to make enough money to purchase huge homes and luxury cars. He lived in a Country Club in Baton Rouge. If you happened to see his house on MTV Cribs, those gold walls were real! I had never seen a black man from the projects live the way he did. The exposure I had to another reality was essential. Legal work that yielded serious dividends. Everything was possible.

I received a call from MTV regarding a sitcom Master P was producing. He'd offered me one of the leading roles. They even sent me the details about the character. I was ready to dive in and live the dream. Unfortunately, Master P later backed out of the deal, and the role never manifested. I was beyond distraught. This could have been my big on-screen break. Now, the opportunity had evaporated, and I was left in the fog of disillusionment.

I lived in Baton Rouge for probably about a year. Even though I was making good money, I got tired of traveling with the crew. I felt as though my dreams were becoming more and more distant. When my lease was up, I went back to Los Angeles again to pursue acting.

In Los Angeles, I got a place in Brentwood with a white guy named Shawn, who became my roommate. Soon after, Cash, my friend from Orleans Parish Prison, moved in with us. There were only four black guys in Brentwood, and Cash and I made up half of them.

I took a job as a night valet at the airport parking cars. Cash worked at a hotel, and Shawn was a massage therapist. With the three of us living in a two-bedroom apartment, we each had money left to spend on good living, nice hotels, elegant restaurants, and interesting women.

Cash was well-spoken and helped connect us with the white community in Brentwood. I guess we were grouped with more of the 'non-threatening' blacks, and the people he introduced us to seemed to love us. When people asked me what university I went to, I told them I attended a small college in Cottonport.

Unfortunately for me, Shawn and Cash were into cocaine and brought many girls to the apartment for crazy parties. I didn't participate in any of their antics because I didn't do drugs anymore. I had long talks with Cash about his drug use, but he ignored any and all of my suggestions. I knew where he was at. He would never listen until he was ready to hear.

Cash hooked up with a brother who worked at the bar at the W Hotel. Every Friday, we had a few drinks at the bar. One night we ran into Jamie Foxx. He'd just had a big movie released right around that time. Jamie bought us a few drinks, and we shared some small talk. Cash told a couple of girls that we were Jamie's security. The next morning, they realized there wasn't a remote chance we were who we claimed to be. We were still three guys living in a two-bedroom apartment.

Chapter 20

SHOWBIZ

I loved my job as a parking attendant and worked hard at it. The job may not have been glamorous, but I made good tips and liked the pace. One night, Cash was invited to a celebrity party in the Hollywood Hills. We all decided to go. I asked for the whole weekend off. Because I had access to all the car keys, I grabbed the keys to Mr. Washington's 500 Mercedes Benz. When Friday night came around, I knew he'd be out of town for the weekend and reasoned I wouldn't get caught. I picked up Cash after work in the Benz and drove up into the Hollywood Hills. Everyone thought we were in the movie business. How easy it was to act the part. I knew I was playing a role. That internal voice that had given me hope in the past was silent now. Perhaps I'd grown a little disconnected from my savior's grace. I was testing the waters of some old and outgrown habits. This wasn't really me, and yet it obviously was.

At the party, Cash started lying about how his dad was a major league baseball player. Cash was the best deceiver I'd ever known. He had lines that he carried around in his pocket–always at the ready. These lies were a double edge sword. Vicky, who owned the house, was a beautiful lady, and her husband, Mr. Adams, worked in the film business. I introduced myself to this beautiful diva in a street-cool way, and we started talking. Cash came over, trying to make a play with the lady of the house. She saw right through him. Cash told her his dad was a professor at the college she attended and then promptly asked for her phone number. Shortly after, her bodyguard escorted us away from her and told us to never speak to her again. The jig was up.

At that party, we also bumped into Tyrese Gibson. He started talking about how he loved the people of New Orleans and had family and close friends from around there. His bodyguard told me, on the side, that Tyrese and I looked alike and that I could probably make a career as his double. He was probably right, but being a body double was not my objective. Cash wanted in on the Hollywood scene by any means necessary. He asked if Tyrese had a personal assistant. Tyrese gave Cash his agent's number. Cash somehow lost the number, and we never saw Tyrese again. I believe it was a Roman philosopher who once said, "Luck is what happens when preparation meets opportunity." Cash had all the drive without any preparation or follow through.

I brought the Benz back to the garage early the next day. My co-worker, Dion, saw me arrive. She said, "Ameer, you better be careful because if you get caught, you could go to jail for taking those people's cars out." She was right, but for some reason, fear didn't stop me from doing the thing I knew could land me back in jail. Taking the Benz could have cost me my job. Other people had done the same thing and taken similar risks, but for me, getting caught with any car that wasn't mine posed a serious risk of going back to prison.

My consciousness was eating me alive. The desire to be rich always pulled at my thoughts. Our Western culture promotes success as material wealth. God was important to me, but He no longer dominated my thoughts. How disappointing that I turned to God when I needed him, then soon after I got what I'd begged for, I walked away from Him in the opposite direction.

Most of the employees at the parking lot were Hispanics. I noticed that they really stuck together. Their main goal was to take care of their families– whether they lived abroad or here in the US. There was a time when Black folks used to be that way too, that is until drugs became more important. Many of the people I'd grown up around started getting high and leaving their kids alone to their own devices. Way too young, kids were exposed to other adults getting high. The combination of being unskilled with the rigors of parenting and fleeting supervision with the availability of street drugs everywhere made for an 'every person for themselves' mentality. Where I grew up, it was hard to get a sixteen-year-old black kid to do an honest day's labor. As kids, we had no work ethic and felt entitled.

For a period in my life, I hung out with a few wealthy women. Like the assistance I'd received from Master P, these generous women provided the financial support I needed so that modeling was no longer a necessity. I could focus solely on my dream of becoming an actor. But morally, things were questionable for me. I didn't feel right about not having my own means to support myself.

Just as things started to look bad, Master P invited me to do a few independent films with him. This was a major blessing because I was running out of money again. He always kept an eye on me and periodically gave me work in his movies.

I was also struggling to find a good agent. Master P hooked me up with Endeavor, one of the top agencies in Los Angeles. At my first audition in 2002, I got a co-lead role in the movie, The New Guy. The three weeks I spent on the set in Austin, Texas, were incredible. Filming with Eddie Griffing was a great experience. My dreams were slowly manifesting.

One night, I was invited to go to a strip club with the film crew. I didn't want to go, but I also didn't want to disappoint the producers or Eddie. Temptation and distraction lurked around every turn. I left the club early with the excuse of an early call for a shoot the next day.

My fear was that something would go wrong. Every time I got closer to my dream, there was a step backward. Maybe this was God's way of reminding me to keep my faith at the forefront of my ambitions. My agent got fired from his firm. Another agent with United Talent Agency, one of the most powerful agencies in the industry, agreed to help me without signing me on. He soon found a TV show audition for me. I studied and prepared the whole night. During the audition, I went blank. It was so embarrassing. I had the same feelings I'd had in my sixth-grade English class in school. A paralysis followed by the shame that my brain couldn't cope with the stress of reading and performing in front of others. I'd memorized my lines, but I was still unprepared for the experience.

Two days later, the producers emailed the agent that I wasn't ready for acting and recommended I find another career. Words can be very powerful, especially when they come from people in positions of power. I was crushed, but I wouldn't let myself walk away from the only dream I had. Success is the award of hard work and dedication. I knew I could work harder, behind the scenes, away from the public eye. All those years I pushed through, the sweat, tears, and blood were my test to see if I still could continue to pursue the dream. The hardest part? When a person is committed enough to still push through the disappointment and rejection the industry brings, and still nothing happens, sometimes for years and years. I knew my passion was there, and I had to believe that my capabilities would soon follow. But when would my day come? When would I finally rise up and shine?

A lady in my apartment complex, who happened to be an acting coach, began teaching me some valuable acting techniques. In 2003, I finally landed a few minor roles in The Handler and the hit show, E.R.

Finally, I got a guest-starring role in The Handler. I was thrilled to be working with Hill Harper. He truly had a divine presence. He was polite, ivy league educated, and professional. He treated me like we were equals. I was still honing my craft, but to him, there was no difference between a lead actor and a guest star.

Hill had money but drove a small, electric car to work every day. Not once did I hear him talking about his affairs with women or indulging in the purchase of extravagant and showy jewelry. He told me about his investments in bed and breakfast establishments. He had just written a book, Letters to A Young Brother: MANifest Your Destiny.

His priorities were greatly different from the rap artists I'd looked up to. As I was exposed to artists and creatives who embraced simplicity and activism over material wealth, I began to realize that rap music can have a dangerous effect on young minds. When gangster rap music is mixed with poverty and uneducated people, the powerful influence can help create potential domestic terrorists. Think about it, those in terrorist organizations are usually disenfranchised, uneducated people, easily brainwashed by those who hold influence. When music is created through the lens of an artist's own trauma and unhealthy vision of self, the adverse effects are obvious. Many of my friends had listened to these songs all day. A person's rage might define their own reality, but not God's. Gospel music and gangster rap come from the same people on opposite ends of inspiration and depravity. Both are reflections of the uplifted and the downtrodden spirit.

Some gangster rappers I knew did good things within their communities, but then they did much more damage with their lyrics. In my hometown, many drug dealers couldn't wait for the latest rap album to drop so they could listen to more songs about drugs and mistreating women. So many men end up in prison, having been influenced by these glorified stories of selling drugs and gaining sexual control in an effort to exert their male prowess. I understand these rappers are often in the business of creating this imagery for the money and the lifestyle, but they often poison young minds in the process. Imagine if the words to these rap songs were more uplifting–like Marvin Gaye, James Brown, and Curtis Mayfield. These musicians inspired people to educate themselves, love themselves, and unite. But some of the lyrics of today are lethal. What about rap songs that educate on social issues instead? Those rap songs exist but are more difficult to sell in the projects. To address the denial of human rights, educational disparities, and the social fallout associated with illiterate men who grow up in poverty and get stuck in the trap of poverty, now that's a beat I can bounce to.

I would never glorify that kind of volatile lifestyle in my chosen profession, and I appreciated seeing Hill Harper's approach to his life and his art form. If the lyrics of a song are damaging to young minds, the money made by the sale of the songs isn't worth it. If I were asked to play a role that was not aligned with my values, I'd turn it down in a heartbeat. I've come a long way, but I feel strongly that a moral and financial match are important to true and lasting success. I still aspire to contribute in a major way to rehabilitating my community. At this time in my life, I wasn't acting on my passions yet, but I was gaining invaluable life lessons that would inevitably help guide me back home. I wanted to help be the change I wanted to see in the projects and beyond.

Chapter 21

LIFE'S MISSION

My ultimate goal was to fight illiteracy, starting with the most critical population of school-aged youth. I headed back to New Orleans in 2003 and got involved with a small youth outreach program for troubled kids. I felt compelled to help the young men of this neighborhood. The program's center was located in a small building on Dry Street.

I had great memories of Dry Street from my childhood. My mother and grandmother would bring us there every year to buy our school clothes. Although we liked our neighborhood, it was always a pleasure to get out of the projects. I enjoyed seeing nice homes and all of the people walking up and down Dry Street.

Back in the day, on Saturday mornings, my grandmother would be out walking around before the blistering sun could burst through the clouds. She had strong legs and an even stronger will–like nothing I have ever seen. Dry Street was quite a walk from the projects where we lived. As a kid, I'd get tired of walking and cry for my grandmother to carry me half the way there. She always did.

The store owners knew my grandmother because she was their housekeeper. She'd always tell us how blessed we were and say, "These are some good white people. They never charge me full price for yall's clothes." I still don't know how we made it off the little money we had, but I never went to bed on an empty stomach, and I always had clean clothes on my back.

As a kid, the projects felt safe, even though they really weren't. Although it was fun to visit these nice neighborhoods, I always couldn't wait to get back home. How amazing, when I look back, how comfortable we were with our own poverty. What becomes normalized can feel safe even when it's actually the opposite.

At the youth program center, these innocent, young kids seemed doomed to failure. There was no real intervention, just four mentors who'd shown up because they cared. We were all former kids from the streets.

I knew what it was to be a victim of street life. I was there to plant any seed of hope I could in these young men. I was there to be the adult I wished I'd seen. Many of their situations were worse than my own upbringing. Some of these kids had no parents at all. Some only had grandmothers who lacked the right tools to raise them.

I gave one of the young men my testimony of how God had allowed me to stand before him and change my life's outcome. They couldn't believe that I'd ever sold drugs, let alone murdered another man as a result of my gangster ambitions. They laughed at the way I spoke now and called me a nerd. I found this quite humorous, considering how hard I'd worked to speak well. Their surprise also saddened me. I spoke in an educated manner that was foreign to them. There was a time when I could relate to their ignorance. I was so grateful for my GED and the effort I'd given to learning to read and write and communicate more intelligently and clearly.

One little kid at the center tried his hardest to look tough and called me all sorts of names. He was the one I directly paid the most attention to and who I tried to help out the most. When a child never receives love, one of the only options available to their young mind is to get attention by acting out. Shame fatigue is real. When you feel shame for long enough, you no longer care what kind of attention you receive, be it negative or positive attention, just that someone sees you at all.

One of the mentors had extensive knowledge of black history. I listened in when he spoke to the kids because I learned so much right along with the rest of our group. They still weren't being taught in school the history that would make them understand just how powerful and full of potential they actually were.

Each week, we taught and coached the kids through different sessions followed by music—usually played by one of the youngsters who were in the process of practicing and pursuing a music career. I appreciated that his lyrics were positive and encouraged him to pursue his rap career in tandem with finishing high school and learning a trade.

For some of these kids, college wasn't a remote possibility. So, if I could encourage them to finish high school, they might have a chance to consider further education. I prayed after each session that these kids would be positively affected by our work and was grateful for the opportunity to have even a small part in influencing their lives.

My passion was to help these young men see life through a different lens. That mission turned out to be challenging because so many different factors came into play. For example, most of their parents didn't have the life skills or the financial means to provide their children with a better life. Some communities had dwindling resources and deplenished budgets, with no playgrounds, no sports programs, or after-school activities available to keep kids occupied and out of trouble. I could also identify all the usual ghetto suspects who so easily disseminated their poisonous message of getting rich quickly by selling drugs. An 'easy' lifestyle with the potential to buy all the things parents couldn't afford would always lure young people before recognizing this sales pitch was nothing but a trap.

I asked myself why it had to be this hard. But God makes no mistakes. This journey, my journey and theirs, was filled with struggles, obstacles, and hardships. These hurdles could kill you or build character–that was up to you. When God gives an assignment, we have to fight to do our homework; we may even have to fight just to stay alive. Many lose their dreams and direction in the face of adversity. Only those who can find a growth mindset, a willing mind, and a strong focus can pierce through the toughest circumstances.

I was trying to instill in these young kids that when things aren't going the way we want or plan or how we think they *should* go, and those we may have shared our dreams with have ridiculed our ambition, our will to reach for something greater can be tested. These challenges can affect our will to persevere, our desire to be good, and distract the clear focus it takes to break away from adversity and keep moving forward toward our potential. My message to them was to disregard those who doubt and to tune out the haters altogether. Negativity is only as attractive as we let it be. Keeping away from those people whose very presence sucks the life out of you was the key to surviving the streets. I tried to preach the importance of surrounding yourself with goal-oriented people who encourage you to succeed and to recognize those who may wish to see you fail because they can't see themselves winning. In the past and still, to that day, I was amazed to have my own so-called friends laugh at me, saying I was crazy for trying to be an actor and a model. I knew firsthand what these kids were up against and how many would try to pull them back down if they dared to climb out.

My old friends did everything in their power to dissuade me from doing what I was called to do. I wish many of them were still alive today to see the successes I have achieved—not to gloat, but to show them what's possible. I wonder what they'd say if they saw me appear on the big screen. I hold no animosity towards those I knew who are either dead now or locked up. They helped me realize so much of my strengths came from my vulnerabilities. We need opposition in life. Sometimes we need to experience what we don't want before claiming what we do. Reaching our full potential is a labor of self-love with lots of trial and error in between. Many people told me my career would never happen, and I said, "Just watch me."

I have read many books about great people who've come through adversity only to prevail. Most of these notable people had similar experiences with other individuals who served as barriers and claimed they couldn't do anything greater. Please don't believe that we only get one chance in life. When we fail at something, we can try a different way, again, and again, and again, and again, and again, until whatever we desire comes to fruition. To fail is natural, essential even, but to be a failure is to become the opposite of what God has invited us to be. Imagine what a heaven on earth we could create if we aspire to embody divine qualities and live like heroes here on earth, helping to lift each other up. We all have the ability to win. With the right tools of support, we can offer each other the gift of rising up.

Chapter 22

HURRICANE KATRINA

The day before Hurricane Katrina made landfall in 2005, my mother, grandmother, and little brother came and asked me to evacuate. It took my mother over an hour to convince me to leave with them. The only reason I agreed to go was to help my mother travel with my grandmother, who had recently developed Alzheimer's. I planned to return the next day.

My mother was very nervous about the storm and wanted to get as far away from New Orleans as possible. We loaded up my mother's little car and left my Expedition parked in the driveway so we could save on gas. It seemed everyone in New Orleans was trying to get to Texas using only a two-lane highway. During the last hurricane, the five-hour drive took about twenty-four hours. So instead, I decided to drive in the opposite direction and headed to Nacadish, Mississippi.

When we were kids, my mother told us about Hurricane Betsy in 1965. That hurricane had killed seventy-six people, and the water level rose twenty feet. Katrina would kill one thousand eight hundred people. My mother knew all too well what was possible if the levees were to break.

We stopped at a Wal-Mart in Franklin, Louisiana for water. I had never witnessed such chaos in my life. People were fighting over resources as if it were armageddon or a post-war situation. People were buying everything they could get their hands on, and the shelves were instantly bare everywhere. The scenes were dire, and I felt as if the world had come to an end.

My grandmother's Alzheimer's made her delusional, and she became paranoid as a result of being in the car for so long. We had to stop regularly in an effort to keep her calm.

When we arrived in Mississippi, there was total confusion about what we'd do next. Our first goal was to secure a place to sleep. All hotels and motels were already full. We drove around to different churches looking for any kind of shelter. Everywhere we went was full and couldn't take us. After riding around for an hour and a half, that same voice inside told me to turn around and check one more time. A small school had been converted to a temporary shelter. I believe my internal guide was God's angel talking to me. My intuition had guided us to safety and just in time.

My mother and family stayed in the car while I checked to see if they would allow us in. Thankfully, they did. We signed in and claimed a place near the door. I helped my grandmother into the gym area and began to get her settled.

The entire scene was depressing. My little brother Ronald, who was thirteen at the time, started complaining about how he didn't want to sleep there. Babies were crying, and children were running around wild. People who had financial security and those who didn't were suddenly all sharing the same sleeping quarters. Somehow, God had let us all know we were equal. On that day, the playing field of class and poverty was as level as I'd ever seen it. When a natural disaster is at play, material possessions no longer matter; everyone just wants to survive.

I was blown away by the locals' generosity. They seemed genuinely glad to have us there and opened their arms and homes to everyone. While my mother was praying outside, a friendly lady named Pat asked her if we needed a place to stay. My mom came inside and asked me to talk to her. After speaking to her for just a few minutes, I gladly accepted her offer to stay with her. We packed up again and drove about two miles to her home. It was a nice, clean house, and we were grateful for our kind host. She was a lifesaver to our family and a godsend in a moment of complete uncertainty and stressful relocation. We were exhausted and soon found ourselves restlessly asleep.

My mother's loud scream woke me up in the middle of the night. I sprinted to the living room towards her voice. Her eyes were locked on images on the television screen. New Orleans, the hometown I loved profoundly, was underwater. What my mother had most feared had finally happened. We all sat in front of the screen until the morning, crying in disbelief. So many had already died, and thousands were stranded. Many people didn't have transportation to leave town, and others just didn't believe this level of catastrophe could happen. I was, at first, reluctant to leave our house as well. I thought I'd wait out the hurricane in the projects with my friends. I was certain that no wind or storm could knock down those bricks in the projects. I thought our neighborhood was somehow indestructible. No one in our circle of neighbors and friends thought about the water level rise completely blowing the levies.

This was all too overwhelming for me. I went out for some fresh air. I met people residing in a motel around the corner from Pat's house. Many of them had lost everything. I went into the reception area to listen in on their conversations.

We shared in each other's anguish. There were people of all colors talking and crying together. Never had I seen black and white people helping and embracing each other in this way, not like this, not on this scale. I thought for a moment that if the world could only remain this way, humans connecting beyond race and status, interconnected communities would transform us all. What a better world we could create, to live side by side, showing greater care for one another. I just wish the moment wasn't full of so much loss of life, for it was a beautiful sight to behold.

Pat's neighbor brought me to a Christian radio station. They had prayed for our family and had gathered a collection for us. At the end of the prayer, a lady I had never met before told me that she'd had a holy message come through to her. God had a ministry waiting for me. She saw me stepping in to change the lives of kids who desperately needed my help. She went on to say how He had souls waiting to hear from me. Young men who needed me were waiting, and I would have to rise to meet them if I wanted to do God's will. I felt the power of God radiating around and through this woman.

Her words, along with the devastation I experienced in those few days after Katrina, rekindled my relationship with God. I felt my calling rise. Even amongst all the death and destruction, communities had bonded and risen up to help one another survive what the devastating waters had wrought. I was ready to heed the call.

My family lost everything during the hurricane. My mother's friend, who lived in Texas at the time, invited our family to stay with her until my mom got back on her feet. A week later, my mother decided to move to Houston. We drove down together, but I felt uncomfortable about moving in with my mom's friend, so I stayed with an old friend of mine for a few weeks instead. After my family was settled in Houston, I headed back to Los Angeles to jump-start my acting career.

People were generous to me during this hard time in my life. I lived at a Days Inn on Sunset Boulevard for a month after arriving back in town. The hotel owners fed me and helped me get in touch with FEMA. I made a desperate call to a friend named Clifton Powell and told him that I was basically homeless and had no clothes. Clifton brought me some clothing and essentials and allowed me to spend quality time with him and his wife. My friend, Faizon Love, let me stay with him for a while, and he introduced me to some other actors.

The acting business was still just as tough as I remembered. This wasn't a nine-to-five job with a fixed salary and benefits. I wasn't in the actors guild just yet. I picked up a couple of TV show roles. I was still paying my dues without a safety net. With acting, even after securing an agent, I still had to compete with dozens of people for the same roles.

Successful acting roles weren't always handed out based on talent. There was a lot of nepotism. I had seen unknown actors run circles around well-established actors–making some of the more famous lead stars look like novices. In my workshop classes, I came across amazing artists who never got their big breaks.

As for myself, I never desired to be famous. My main motivation became my desire to utilize acting as a platform to talk to kids and men behind bars. I wanted to make good on the calling I'd had after Katrina. I was determined to shine a bright light on what life could be like beyond the barriers of shame. I had emancipated myself from a dealer's life that was designed for failure. I had shed my shame and traded my pain for hope.

Chapter 23

BROKEN HEART

Kim and I grew up together in the New Orleans projects. We ran into each other again in 2004, when we both lived in New Orleans. She had two children, and their father was a popular, successful, wealthy rapper. He was a controlling man who didn't really spend time with his family. Kim told me he was there for the family financially but that their relationship was often unstable. Some parents try to substitute money for love. Unfortunately, Kim's kids missed out on a father who could have given them what they really wanted–him in their lives.

Kim was a loving and caring woman. She provided some of the motivation and inspiration I needed in my life. I loved her and found it hard to stay away from her. I had fallen in love with this special person. This was real love. I was trying to get her to leave this guy, the father of her children, and be in a committed relationship with me instead. I had already gotten attached to her kids. I really thought she could have been the one I'd been searching for.

There were times when we went out, and people would comment on how beautiful my family was. They weren't my family, but they made me feel complete, and that's all I'd ever wanted in my life, to create in adulthood what I'd missed in my childhood. I think every man can benefit in his soul from the experience of having a family. I believe that's what God intended, for us to fully embrace raising children and having a partner in this life to share the experience of parenting. Every kid needs two consistent figures in their young lives and parents who, ideally, live in the same house peacefully. Good parenting takes skill, and it helps to have backup.

I knew I was getting in deeper. For the first time in my adult life, I took on the responsibility of being a father figure and felt the skill and commitment the role required. I took them to the park and the movies–even when I was exhausted and didn't have much energy left to give, I prioritized their needs over my own. I loved baking cookies with them and playing games. I would act like a monster and chase them around the house–by far, the best acting job in the world. The kids never said anything to their biological dad about my relationship with their mother. Kim's daughter, Tia, told me she wished I'd been her dad all along, and her son, Liam, would ask why I couldn't be his dad right now.

When I had my own home with my own family, I dreamt about how I'd make sure that every kid in my neighborhood knew they had a safe place to rest, anytime, any day, at my house. I had the pressing compulsion to be a father figure to as many kids as needed. I knew firsthand how many children back home would never know a father's love.

Liam was a good kid and extremely shy. I showed this little guy how to brush his teeth properly and floss thoroughly. I showed them what my family hadn't shown me. I helped to build his confidence with long talks and encouragement. When he signed up for flag football for the first time, the father never attended any of his games. His dad obviously didn't understand the value of supporting his children by showing up. Money alone cannot raise well-adjusted children. Kids want more than anything for their dad to show up and root them on–whatever they happen to be doing or playing or performing. In fact, money can be a barrier when substituted for the physical contact kids crave and only receive when their parents are fully present. His son preferred love and support over everything else. I enjoyed nourishing this boy, and I hoped someday he'd have the skills to do the same for his future children.

Tia loved it when I came to town. She enjoyed listening to the stories I told her at bedtime. These children taught me that kids do not understand the value of money until they're much older. From a very young age, what they do understand is the importance of feeling loved. I had so much love to give to these kids. I was ready to give a million times more love than I had received. I wanted them to feel valued and seen.

I loved those kids like they were my own, and I often wished they were. I desperately desired to know what it would be like to be a father. I found myself acting like a father figure, teaching them about black history, math, and vocabulary. Their aunt had just died in a car accident, and they had so many questions. We took long walks, discussing the love of God and where people go after they die. They sometimes asked, "…why doesn't Daddy live with us, and how come he likes another lady instead of Mommy?" These questions broke my heart, but they were for their father to answer. In the meantime, I would be there to fill the role of a loving father figure.

After Hurricane Katrina, Kim moved to New York City. I traveled to New York every chance I got. My relationship with the kids and Kim remained strong even though I was back and forth.

New York was a beautiful place to visit. Whenever I had a break, I'd fly out to see them. Kim decided to move to a new condo on the beach in the Hamptons for the summer, and I flew in to help her get settled. It was always good to see the kids, and I missed them terribly when I wasn't with them.

Kim's ex was due back in town for a day. He was coming by the house to ensure the new furniture he bought had been delivered. I left the house to avoid meeting him.

The next day the kids wanted to go swimming. I brought my book and relaxed while the kids played in the water. As the waves crashed on the sand, I smelled the ocean and appreciated how blessed I was to be living like this. Like many of my friends, I could have been high on drugs, in jail, or dead. I didn't take one day of my freedom for granted.

As I read my book, I realized the neighbors' curious eyes were staring at me. These were million-dollar condos the kids and I sat in front of. I guess they might have thought any muscular black man hanging out on their beach was most likely an athlete–maybe a pro football or basketball player. I have always been struck by how people associate success with geography; they'll often think a person is 'somebody' if they're in proximity to other people with money. I seemed to stick out and fit in all at once only because I looked up to par with the locals. I may have been a black brother from the projects, but I still had a toned body and white teeth, so I passed for someone who belonged there.

People with money in the Hamptons knew how to use it, but I cannot lie, I too, enjoyed the luxuries that came with wealthy living. Kim and I often stood out on the balcony at her condo, watching the endless blue ocean and feeling the summer breeze on our skin. I felt so much gratitude that she had shared all this comfort and easy living with me. The life I'd known in the projects was very different from this experience. I thought about how many inner-city kids had never experienced playing on a beach quite like this one.

Kim was a wonderful mother and a great human being. In addition, my mother liked her, which was a big deal to me. We talked about building a future together and expanding our family with a child of our own. My heart and soul were fully invested in this vision. I dreamt about holding our future baby, my baby, in my arms and reading good night stories to our newborn.

That summer, Kim decided to get out of her entire situation with the kid's father. She wanted to make their separation official. I wanted to believe her, that she'd finally commit to separating herself completely from this man. I wanted to trust her highest intentions, even though I knew she was scared to leave her financial security and this comfortable lifestyle behind.

The next time her ex came to the house, he showed up in a rage because he'd finally figured out that Kim and I were in a serious relationship. When he banged on the door, I went to the kid's room to avoid him and any possible conflict.

When I heard Kim yell out in pain, I rushed toward the living room. His hands were around her neck, and he was choking her. I threw the first punch to get him off of her and began beating him with blows landing left and right. Imagine his surprise when I came out of nowhere to defend Kim. He'd had no idea I was even there. He ran towards the door to escape me.

All the while, his kids screamed and cried. He paid no attention to them and couldn't get out of the house fast enough. When he hurriedly flung the door open to leave, his cousin was standing just outside on the porch. In an instant, I recognized his cousin from my prison days. His cousin knew that I was not the type of guy anyone should choose to fight in hand-to-hand combat.

Shortly after, he and his cousin returned to the condo with a posse of guys. Kim called 911, and luckily, the cops arrived fast. The police began to question Kim's ex about the events that had occurred. The kids' father said he'd lost a piece of jewelry during the brawl and told the cops that he just wanted his jewelry back and then he'd leave. There was no way I was going to let him distract the police from what really happened. I asked Kim to come over and show the cops the bruises that had already begun to form on her neck. Her ex was promptly cuffed and taken to jail for assault and battery. Domestic violence is so destructive to everyone involved, especially the children who witness their parents being physically violent with one another. I tried to comfort the kids, but they were badly shaken by witnessing the confrontation.

That night, Kim wanted to pack up everything and leave with me. Although this was the decision I wanted her to make, I also wanted her to make that decision from a peaceful state of mind, not as a reaction to this most recent violent event and the emotional fallout that accompanied her ex's attack.

A few days later, I ran into Kim's ex's bodyguard, who'd been there during the fight and witnessed what had transpired. He gave me a high five and praised me for what I did to protect Kim from his boss. I cannot imagine having someone I trusted in my employ, someone who was supposed to protect *me*, be so glad when someone stepped in and kicked the boss' ass. I think that says a lot about who he was as a person. Even his bodyguards thought he deserved my intervention to stop him. I had sworn off the kind of violence I'd witnessed in prison, but this was a matter of Kim's safety. I didn't have to think twice before stepping in.

After that incident, the kid's father began to further distance himself from his children. The night of the fight, when he saw his daughter in my arms, he said that the children must be mine, not his. He acted so mean towards his daughter, yelling and swearing, "You love Ameer more than me? How could you run into his arms and not mine?" His jealousy, insecurity, and inability to be a good father were on full display.

Witnessing their mother's physical and emotional abuse and our fight affected the kids, and their grades began to drop in school afterward. They had grown up in a pleasant, wholesome environment and weren't accustomed to seeing such violence. I noticed what that single incident had invoked in them and thought about all the kids in the projects who experience that same level of violent chaos every day of their lives.

Kim told me her ex, the manipulator that he was, had started trying to win her back. He asked why she was still messing around with me, noting that I was not a millionaire. He couldn't figure out why she'd be attracted to someone without the kind of money he had. Why would she waste her time? Kim handled the situation well, but I knew she was under a lot of stress. Whenever I was at the house, he'd call at all hours of the night, asking the kids if I was there. I was so mad that he'd involve his children and would dare to question them about my whereabouts. Like many manipulative and abusive men, he'd tell them all kinds of crazy stories about their mom over the phone, even calling them profane names and being continuously aggressive and inappropriate.

I believe deep down, Kim knew that being with me would provide a happier life for her and the kids. However, she had become accustomed and attached to the exquisite lifestyle her ex could provide, and she knew I could not compete, at least not yet, or match his financial support.

More and more, I began to question Kim's ability to maintain any good reason. Knowing more now about the psychology of domestic violence and abuse, I can understand why she remained so attached to this guy. He was the father of her children, and he still held sway over her emotions. I began to suspect Kim had no plans to become financially independent and lacked a certain drive needed for her life to change. I tried my best to help her see that she could have gone back to school or maybe even opened up a small business of her own. From my vantage point, she had no desire to do the hard work that big change requires. The risk and disruption to her kids' lives were more than she could justify. Her decision not to free herself from his hold came with great risk to herself and the kids. Once her youngest child turned eighteen, I could foresee her ex cutting her off entirely and her ending up completely broke. She didn't own her house, and the truck she drove wasn't even in her name. This rapper had complete control over everything in her life, and he wasn't going to relinquish that power easily.

I couldn't help who I fell in love with, and I was truly in love with Kim. I adored her, but I knew this relationship wasn't healthy, and this couldn't be what God wanted for me. I wanted to establish my own family unit. But first, I needed a full commitment from the woman I so desperately wanted to be partnered with.

We'd had five years together, and I never thought our relationship would ever end. I was living in New Orleans and working with students when I received a phone call from her. Kim was pregnant. I could tell her joy wasn't the same as mine, and there was a little reluctance in her voice. She sent me a photograph of the sonogram.

Finally, I'd have my own child to raise, educate and nurture. On my first visit back to New York after the big news, we talked about baby names. I loved rubbing her belly and talking to our future baby. I always wanted to go to the doctor with her for her appointments, but for some reason I didn't understand at the time, she never let that happen.

The second time I tried to visit her after she was pregnant, she told me it was bad timing. A few weeks later, I jumped on a plane to New York; I couldn't wait any longer to see her. As soon as I arrived, the moment I saw her, I instantly knew that she had done the unthinkable and had an abortion. I felt unimaginable grief and immeasurable pain.

I did not have a say in the matter, and she'd already decided for both of us. I believed in a woman's right to choose, yet I was the father of that fetus, and I'd already proven how much I loved her and her entire family. I was ready to hold her hand through sickness and health until death do us apart. We had planned for that future. I didn't understand why she made this decision…alone and without me.

I was devastated by the pain of the loss of my potential little Ameer–a child in my image. The unexpected shock of her betrayal was overwhelming. For her, this pregnancy would have produced her third child. For me, losing the opportunity to have our first child together was too much for my heart to stand.

The news profoundly hurt my family. I was the only one of my siblings who hadn't had a child of my own. My family was upset with Kim for being secretive and deciding not to have another child, our child, without first being honest with me.

My father revealed to me later, and rather bluntly, that when my mother had been pregnant with me, they had also decided she would get an abortion. The reality was they didn't want, nor could they afford, a third child. She was still a child herself, a teenager having babies she would struggle to raise. My mother took two shots to try to bring on a miscarriage but to no avail. I suppose I was stubbornly tenacious even before I was born.

The loss of this potential life, while simultaneously losing the love of my life, was almost too much to bear. My two beautiful gems were suddenly missing. I suffered in silence. The shame that came along with my vulnerability felt wholly tragic. I reasoned that I couldn't share my pain with others—especially in relation to other men—due to the pitiful belief that my loss would somehow make me look like a weaker man. I didn't want to reveal how I'd crumbled under the weight of losing what I thought I'd had before I ever really had anything to call my own in the first place.

I was still emotionally raw, but I needed to forgive Kim and move forward to free myself from the pain of this unbearable disappointment. Kim was used to a victim mindset and sometimes operated from a place of fear and low self-esteem. It was important for me to recognize my own role in our relationship and gain control of my emotions. I did not want to be stuck in a codependent relationship without enough room for both of us to fully grow. Over the years, I've often thought about Kim's kids, who I still love dearly. I wonder how my influence played out in their lives—if they still remembered me or had good childhood memories of our time together.

I knew that Kim could never be a part of my life again. No matter how hard that reality was to swallow, I needed to practice what I preached. I tried to teach my students about how making great choices could influence the outcome of their lives. How could I move forward with Kim and keep pursuing a relationship that could never be all I wanted? I knew staying with her would be the wrong choice. I had to make better decisions that were good for my overall being and aligned with who I'd become as a person. I couldn't settle for a portion of the life I wanted. I had to be an active participant in co-creating with my creator the absolute best life I could. In pursuing only what mattered most, no matter how hard it was, I could be a better version of myself and keep growing toward my potential.

This painful experience with Kim brought back the haunting memories of that agonizing day in the projects where I'd shot and killed another human being. In an instant, it hit me; he was someone's son. I could finally grasp the unbearable pain parents felt–the pain of losing a part of you. I thought about Tim's mother and the agony my actions must have caused her. I reached out to her through mutual acquaintances with the hope that I could apologize for my fatal mistake. I desperately wanted to make amends and account for the pain I had caused her and her family. She responded that she didn't want to meet me in person but that she had been following my career over the years, was proud of the man I had become, and kept me in her prayers. I appreciated her grace more than I could ever convey. I was forever in her debt.

Chapter 24

FAMILY REUNION
BEHIND BARS

Two days before Thanksgiving, 2009, all my immediate family flew to Los Angeles to be with Dash's family. At the last minute, I decided to join the reunion festivities and booked a flight to Los Angeles. Traveling around the holiday season is the most exciting time for me. I love watching people at the airport and all the effort family members make trying to get to their final destination. People are usually smiling joyously at the thought of being with their loved ones, and they seem more willing to converse than at any other time of the year.

Dash picked me up from the airport. He was thrilled about the entire family being reunited. I got excited too, but then I thought about my dad. I secretly hoped that he'd magically decide to appear and make our family feel complete again.

My mother was happy to have all her kids around her. We ate, danced, and jokingly talked and laughed around the table about the good old days. Everyone was quick to remind me of how I used to always pick fights with other kids. Leave it to family members to remind you of who you used to be. They'd never let me forget my bad behavior. My siblings and I were concerned. My mother had gained tremendous weight, so we all got on her and expressed our desire for her to be healthy. I think she actually enjoyed our attention and concern. We had an amazing time.

Two days later, we visited my dad in Lompoc Federal Prison in California. My mother talked about how we could have had a better life the whole ride.

I didn't want to talk about the what-ifs of the past. I was focused on making the most out of my present.

When we arrived at the prison, a familiar feeling encompassed my mind, body, and soul. I dreadfully recalled my days in prison. I had a full-body, somatic reaction to being anywhere close to those walls.

My dad came out smiling and happy to see the faces of those of us who still cared about him. As I watched my mother gaze at her only husband, I could tell she still had love for this man. Like Kim, even though he had abused her and walked out on her and her kids, she still had affection for him. My dad asked my mother when she was going to lose some weight. My mother laughed and asked when he would stop wasting his life away in prison.

My sister was somehow calm during our visit. I was surprised she was able to remain so composed due to how she really felt about our parents. She still held a lot of animosity toward them.

The intergenerational trauma was palpable. It was Dash's young son's first visit to a prison. He was looking around, confused by the whole experience and everything he saw. He wanted to know when my dad was going to be released. My dad responded that he had five more years until he could be free. May his grandson never know his fate, I silently thought. May we somehow break the cycle of incarceration in our family and make sure my nephew had all the early childhood reading intervention he needed, especially if he showed ANY signs of reading difficulties.

I bought my dad hot wings and a Coke from the vending machine. We talked about his friend who'd recently died of cancer. His friend's passing had hit him pretty hard. Later in our conversation, he revealed that he was also dealing with a cancer diagnosis. He told us that his simple wish was to be 'us' again, for our family to be all together, with him being a free man, before cancer took him.

I stared at my dad and his desperation over still being locked up. I asked him about the guy sitting at the next table who looked around my age. My dad told me that this guy had a life sentence. As I stared over at this brother, I realized how easily he could've been me. As I scanned around the visitation room, it was depressing to see all those black men locked up.

I wondered how many of these men could read. The new slavery was educational inequity. Each one of these inmates had a lengthy sentence. Each one of these men, young and old, had a family and a lifetime of limitless potential that had gone unfulfilled.

In a single moment, their unwritten futures turned on a dime. Like me, most of them committed their crimes when they were far too young for impulse control. Our prefrontal cortex in our brain isn't done developing until age twenty-five. Many of the men in our society were committing crimes before their brains had a chance to mature. Lives upon lives snuffed out for what? I knew their stories and the split-second decisions they'd made. I knew the violent inheritance built on broken homes that sat on a foundation of illiteracy and failed academics. I saw a room full of unfulfilled ambitions and the hardness of men that results from debilitating experiences of not knowing where you belong. The negative influences, the guns in young hands, the drugs that numbed–their shame was the pain I could see from across the room–as if it were my own.

My mother started thanking God for all her children being free. She was so grateful we hadn't ended up like my dad, wasting away, estranged from those who knew and loved us. Then my dad expressed his compunction for walking out on us and getting locked up for all these years. We could all see my mother was hurting as we witnessed her tears, the years of worry that had created every line on her beautiful face.

We held each other's hands, crying together. The moment was seared into my memory, and the feeling of acknowledgment of what was and what could have been was devastating and cathartic all at once. It was a special time that I will never forget. My nephew told his grandfather he couldn't wait for him to get out so they could play together. As we left the visitation room, for the first time in my life, I saw my dad cry. My heart broke for him, and I felt so bad for the choices he'd made and all the ways he was alone. There was nothing I could do but be a different man. The car was quiet on the ride back home. We all had a lot to think about.

Chapter 25

PAY IT FORWARD

Even after all my post-traumatic stress from my own education, I found myself a position that put me right back in the school system. How things had changed. I began working with the youth program. The program's focus was to help significantly reduce suspensions and expulsions and increase attendance at Booker T. Washington High School. Students who got kicked out of other public schools ended up in Booker T. Washington, an alternative charter school in New Orleans, a five-minute walk from the Calliope Projects where I grew up. This school was the last stop before expulsion. Consequently, the student body consisted of the wildest and most behavior-challenged students in the area.

After stops and starts, the program was finally approved for more funding and got off the ground. When we first started teaching, there were only three teachers: Cynthia, Cadillac, and me. We were all ex-offenders, and we knew the streets and the kids that offended on those streets all too well. The three of us developed a strategy. Cadillac played the good cop, I played the bad cop, and Cynthia provided the motherly influence. Cadillac was an older guy in his fifties, but he carried himself like a young guy. I still looked youthful enough to gain the kid's trust.

The program began to yield great results, and our methodology was eventually integrated into the school system. There were no other alternative programs being offered to these kids. Our focus was on the four tenants we used: Belonging, Independence, Mastery, and Generosity. They knew this was their last educational option and that we were the only game in town.

Even though we were 'accepted,' there was still some resistance to the program. After all, we were all ex-cons. Many believed we were con artists trying to get money instead of actually helping the kids in our program turn their lives around. Many parents weren't happy that ex-cons were in charge of teaching their children anything. We were called by every name in the book; unfortunately, not the good book. We were under scrutiny, and our qualifications and motives were questioned. To us, we had the best preparation and qualifications possible. We'd already lived what these kids were experiencing on a daily basis.

During the first three months of my time with the program, each day was a living nightmare. Many kids came in high and on pills. When I was in school, I'd done all the same things, so I tried to be patient and accept them for who they were and what they were going through. The kids were so accustomed to having no consequences for their actions that they freely used vulgarity and sometimes violence toward teachers and staff. Things were different when I was a student. On those rare occasions I was physically on campus or in the classroom at school, if a student used that type of language in class, let alone to a teacher, their language would have resulted in an automatic suspension or expulsion.

One of my most effective tools with the kids was to lighten their moods. We knew that if we could get the kids to laugh, we could get their attention. Upon entering the class, we asked the kids' names and how they felt that day. I sang a good morning song every morning. Even the most reluctant students usually joined me. Music is universal, and in this case, I tried to pick songs that would lift their souls.

I began to teach the Cognitive Behavior Therapy class, a new class for the school system and one I wish I'd had access to when I was young. I emphasized to the students the importance of positive thinking and good values and illustrated examples of how to control their thoughts and make better choices. One thing we stressed to the kids was that not every thought or opinion we hold is 'right.' Many of these kids only knew how to think negatively. Although our brains are wired to dwell on the negative, our challenge was to help the kids recognize the difference between positive and negative thinking and how to develop their growth mindset potential. To instill positive values and a cup-half-full mindset was no easy task.

The first couple of months were like pulling teeth. Convincing them to come out of the hallways and into our class was obviously not going to be easy. I often felt sorry for the other teachers who got beaten up by these same students. Many white teachers from good families and different neighborhoods weren't accustomed to this barbaric kind of behavior. Once students sensed fear in their teachers, they could eat them alive. I think the white teachers had a harder time controlling black students with behavior problems. Racial dynamics amongst students and teachers couldn't be dismissed. Black students disrespected these white teachers more than black teachers.

When the kids came into our class, we'd ask them what caused them to act that way. These kids disrupted their classes because they lived by the rules of the streets. We were trying to demonstrate to them that there was a different way to deal with conflict. Conflict resolution tools weren't just a foreign concept to them, they'd never even thought of de-escalating conflicts at all. The adults in their lives didn't model these skills. How could we expect them to know how to do things they'd never seen implemented. We tried to instill in them that they didn't have to fight every time someone said something they didn't like. There were many ways to transform violence.

This one kid, Kindell, would say some of the nastiest things. All of the kids were scared to death of Kindell. He targeted both the staff and myself, calling us names and cursing us out just before bursting out of class. He even called his own mother horrible names in front of the principal. He once said that if I had a daughter, he would rape her. With him, the severity of his volatile language demonstrated the level of his internal pain.

Thinking of Kim's daughter, Tia, and what he said made me have my own violent thoughts. Thankfully, my brain had time to mature. I was in control of my thoughts and actions and didn't react to his vile words. He must have felt horrible about himself to say such things to someone else.

He was the one I'd have to give the most attention to. He was the one who was in the greatest amount of pain and would take the most time and patience to help.

Teaching was a constant struggle. I couldn't tolerate kids using foul language and profanity. I had to send some of the kids out of my class. Soon after, they always wanted to come back in and participate in whatever we were doing. There was always a lot of excitement in my class, and the kids didn't want to miss out on our fun. To be able to return to my class once they'd been asked to leave, they had to apologize for any rudeness, not only to me but to all of the students in the class. That was my rule.

As anyone would suspect, I found many of the most difficult kids had uneducated parents who may have already been incarcerated or caught up in the prison system. Sadly, these parents had already given up on their children. Their parents had little insight on how to nurture a child into a socially and emotionally intelligent member of society. I remember a smart boy in my class who had explosive rage and anger management issues. When I gave him an answer he didn't like, my response would set him off into a frenzy. One day, when we called his dad to the school because of a fight, I had the opportunity to talk with him at length. I informed him of his child's attitude at school and advised him to put his arms around him and tell him that he loved him. One look at this young man and anyone could see his desperation to be loved. When I told his father that this emotional reassurance was what his son was really longing for, I could see his father's face change. Although I felt out of place for saying something to this parent, I took a gamble and ultimately won. His dad responded by saying that he'd try the approach I'd recommended. Imagine having to 'try' to put your arms around your kid and tell him that you love him.

After that conversation, I wanted to shout from the rooftops all across the projects, "Hug your children!" Every time a kid leaves for school, parents need to say, "I love you," squeeze them tight and show their children how much they are loved. I wish these words were universal and weren't a strenuous task for anyone to say. Unconditional love is a powerful salve to a wounded society. We need to practice until we are able to say words of affection effortlessly. And yet, there I was telling a father to tell his boy he loved him.

Our only goal of the program was to introduce these kids to pro-social values: love, trust, peace, faith, forgiveness, and humility. Channel 4 News came to the school because the program had noticeably reduced suspensions and expulsions. In the news segment, the reporter introduced me as a murderer because of the crime I'd committed when I was only fourteen and the actor from the hit HBO show, Treme. Oddly enough, this reporter mentioned Treme even though I had only recently auditioned for the show, and I hadn't yet heard back from casting if I'd even gotten the part. Regardless, I was more than willing to use my platform to draw attention to the good effects the program was having on our city's youth.

I explained how we worked in this school for three months without pay. My heart was in making a real difference in these kids' lives. We were all dedicated and serious about helping our students stay in school and out of trouble. There were still too many killings going on, and the schools were too rowdy for students to learn. These kinds of programs and interventions weren't just necessary, they were essential if we were to make a dent in the crime and murder rates of our city. If not now, then when, and if not me, then who? I was not going to sit by and watch another generation get wiped out.

Shortly after the reporter mistakenly referred to me as the actor from Treme, I got a callback and was indeed cast on the show. My role was as an Indian Chief's son who didn't want to stay in New Orleans after Hurricane Katrina. The role lasted two weeks and was filmed right in my own city. I was super excited that I could do both of the things I loved, acting and teaching, at the same time.

After the HBO show, my agent started calling me daily, asking me to return to California. My resume had grown, and she thought I had a good shot at becoming an in-demand actor. Fame and money weren't my main objectives. I truly enjoyed my work with the kids. Plus, I already felt like a star. Coming from prison to making a living in the movie business, I considered myself a success story.

I was offered a small role on a TV show. The money was good, but the job was on the West Coast. I thought about the kids, and I knew that I couldn't leave them in the middle of the school year. The bonds I had built with the students had become too strong to jeopardize. Many of the girls, some of whom were teenage moms, started to open up to me about the sexual abuse they'd already experienced in their young lives. One of my students, Jermaine, was a drug dealer and had recently been arrested. He was going back and forth to court. I became close with Jermaine. He sometimes stayed at my house. I took him to Tulane University in an effort to open his eyes to the opportunities that awaited him if he could find the strength to make better choices. One day, while driving together in the car, he told me that he'd never forget me. This brought tears to my eyes. Since I got out of prison, my main objective was to one day impact young black lives. This was the best reward I could have imagined.

I taught six classes every day, and each class had about ten kids in attendance. The kids had issues ranging from a complete lack of parental supervision or guidance to substance abuse and a history of sexual abuse. Most of the time, I couldn't help but take their problems home with me. The deep sense of sadness and empathy I felt for these students was too real. I was invested in every one of their lives and in all their, often tragic, stories. As a result, I became extremely depressed at times. I would ruminate and question how parents could subject their children to all the things these kids told me they were going through. How could a child fully function knowing that their parents were crack-heads or that they lacked any basic parenting skills at all? I reckoned that black families in our neighborhoods were in a moral, social and economic crisis.

When I was in school, mothers would believe any teacher who told them a story regarding what their kids were *really* up to. I saw a change in today's parents, who wouldn't hear of their child being guilty of anything. Whatever happened was never their fault, and no one was culpable. I had a hard time finding parents who took responsibility for the harshest realities of what these kids were doing and what was being done to them. Many of my students could make better choices if there were examples of any good role models in their households. The only resolution to this epidemic was for parents to take responsibility for their own actions so their kids would see how it's done. Kids emulate what they see. We must be concerned about our children, their best friends, and even our neighbor's kids in our communities. Inside healthy communities, it doesn't just take a village to raise conscientious and well-adjusted human beings. In this modern era, it might just take an educational revolution.

After class one day, a student left me an anonymous letter on my desk. "If you touch one person's life here, today, you touch the world."

This note so moved me because it seemed that I had gotten through to this child. Again I thought about Kim's kids, and I hoped they would hold on to all of the conversations we had about life choices and the positive values I tried to exemplify.

These kids were hungry to learn and have any positive reinforcement directed their way. I could see this desire for acceptance and praise whenever I would tell them that I appreciated their behavior. Other kids would say, "What about me? Do you like how I'm behaving in school, Mr. Ameer?" They were eager for positive reinforcement through my undivided attention. I was more than happy to give them exactly what they craved.

A lot of my students were on medications such as Prozac to stabilize their mood or Adderall to calm down their hyperactivity. Dewight was a new student who had just enrolled in my class. He was transferred in from another school because he'd stabbed a teacher with a pencil. I asked what his name was and where he'd come from. He started yelling and calling me a fag. He shouted that I sounded like a white man, and he asked if I was gay. I guess he was trying to demonstrate his manhood by rebelling against me. In an effort to prove his sexuality, he thought he had to question mine.

I was wounded to see so many talented kids waste their lives. Every day on the New Orleans news, they reported young teens being gunned down. If only the things I was teaching at school could be taught at home, violence would be in decline. But too many parents were sitting at home collecting government checks while their kids were busy committing heinous crimes and terrorizing their teachers in the public school system or in their neighborhoods.

One month before summer vacation, I was walking through the lunch line in a narrow hallway. A kid smacked me on the head as I passed him. I had no idea who it was. When I turned around and asked who did it, a student affiliated with the infamous Birdman gang said, "Nigga, I did it, and whatcha gonna do?"

Still, my innate reaction was to knock him out. As my mentor, the old man in prison taught me, one must become a disciple of their thoughts and values. This philosophy helped me change my path, and violence was no longer part of my value system, so I restrained myself. I had to be an example of what I was so desperately trying to introduce to these kids. Per school policy, I had the right to put him in his place, but I chose to walk him to the principal's office instead. I reported him to the principal, and he was suspended for five days. When his parents came to school, I realized that his mother and I had been in some of the same classes and had gone to school together.

I talked with my students about the decision I'd made not to retaliate and hit this kid after he'd hit me first. This situation was not life-threatening. I was asking these kids to learn earlier what I wished I'd known before the streets began to dictate my behavior. They said, "But Mr. Ameer, he put his hands on you. He disrespected you!" They told me I should have beaten him up in return. I told them that if I'd done that, I might have been fired, and I wouldn't have been acting on my values, which were more about granting forgiveness rather than experiencing the temporary satisfaction of hurting someone who has offended me.

I was sitting with a few security guards on campus during lunch break one day. One of the guards, who I had grown up with in the projects, mentioned that he'd heard about the student who'd hit a teacher. When I told him I was the teacher, he was shocked. He said, "Millie, nigga, you've really changed! When we were coming up, nobody dared put their hands on you." The rest of the security guards didn't understand the context because I no longer carried myself as a violent person. Only the people who'd known me when I was younger realized how much I had rehabilitated my behavior. After being released from prison, I recreated myself.

A few days later, I was asked to intervene with a few teenagers who'd participated in a gun battle–another unsolved shootout in the projects.

When I arrived, I recognized one of the kids as the student who'd hit me while we were standing in the lunchline. He was from the Birdman gang, and I could see he was well armed and carrying a gun. I knew that if I had hit him back in the lunchline, he probably would have tried to kill me right then and there.

Honestly, I used to be just like him. When I was his age, and I'd held the power of a gun in my hands, I would have done the same thing. That was the code of the projects. An eye for an eye. Someone hits you, and you hit back. When kids hit back with bullets instead of fists, the consequences of poor judgment are much more permanent.

Chapter 26

ALTERNATIVE
TO THE STREETS

A key contributor to the program, Khalil Osirius, was conducting a golf tournament fundraiser to buy curriculum and books for the children participating in Cognitive Behavior Therapy.

On the day of the tournament, one hundred and fifty people attended the event. At hundred-fifty dollars per ticket, the proceeds rolled in. Even some of our students were in attendance. In the end, aside from some hiccups, the event was a total success.

After the event, I gave Jermaine a ride home. We stopped at McDonald's, and he opened up to me about his problems at school and at home. With tears in his eyes, he told me that his mother was currently being pulled out of the projects because his brother was busted selling drugs from their family home.

Jermaine was worried that his mother wouldn't be able to make ends meet. He considered selling drugs again to help his family from becoming homeless. I knew all too well about the frustration in his life, so I tried to help him focus on the positive things that were still within his control. I reframed and illustrated his future so he could avoid having to live it. I told him that he should try to find legitimate work instead of selling dope and that if he were selling drugs, he would most likely end up in a worse situation and be arrested. If that happened, who would take care of his mother?

His two brothers were already in jail for murder and heroin charges. I told him that he had to be the one sibling to take a different path and carve an altogether different road in the opposite direction. He told me that every day was a bad day for him and his mother. His story broke my heart because his household situation was desperate. His house was filthy, and there was no food in the refrigerator. He must have felt like he had no other choice. But I was there to tell him there was always another choice.

Jermaine's mother didn't work, nor could she read. I discovered this fact when I brought Jermaine on the set of Treme as an extra. His mother had to fill out the paperwork to grant permission for him to hang out on set with me. The form contained basic information such as his name, address, and date of birth. She confided in me that she couldn't write.

David was another student who was friends with Jermaine. I took both of them on the set with me, and they were cast as extras in one of the episodes. They played the part of family members and friends during a scene. It was good to see these young men dressed up in their wardrobe of tailored suits during the funeral scene. They seemed proud and completely changed as they donned their character's clothes. David had decided he wanted to get into acting after finishing his scene. Both of these boys were eventually featured in a PBS episode about the youth program.

I started picking David up two days a week to teach him cold reading and scene study. I had learned these techniques in acting school. David could read well and was catching on really fast. But I couldn't pull him away from the dangerous groups of kids he associated with on the weekends. I taught David about negative social interaction. The likelihood of mirroring what your peers do is so great at that age, whether the given action happens to be positive or negative. I could sense that peer pressure might be his downfall.

Devastatingly, David and his friends went out one Friday night and gang raped a white woman. The story was all over the news. This kid had so much potential. He was a nice-looking kid with a baby on the way. David was sixteen, and the DA wanted to charge all of the boys who were a party to the rape charges as adults. If found guilty, he could spend the rest of his life in jail. He might never be granted the opportunity to see his child grow up.

Another baby having babies, and another absentee father in the making. The teachers and principal all came together and prayed. He ended up receiving a twenty-year sentence for the violent crime he'd committed. Twenty years of his life gone, just like that.

On the other hand, Jermaine was still in school while also pursuing a rap career. I believed this was one kid whose life I had already impacted. He could be one of the lucky few to redefine his odds. He was no longer into drugs, and he was well on his way toward a new path. I was there to keep encouraging and inspiring him.

Many people left this community, sought their fortunes, maybe even became wealthy, and then never returned. After two years of trying to get Master P to visit our alma mater, his publicist finally called me back one day to tell me he was interested in coming for a visit. I had been determined to get him in front of these students. I felt like the kids needed to see him, hear his story, and recognize his humble beginnings. I wanted them to be encouraged. They would hear a story of redemption from a multi-millionaire who'd been able to navigate the streets and then enjoy a lifestyle every one of my students coveted.

Master P came in with four vans filled with security guards and boxes of t-shirts for each and every kid. It had been two years since we last met. I told him about how extreme many of the kid's situations were and how great it would be for him to talk about his struggles growing up, in a two-bedroom home, with ten people living there.

I called all the news channels to let them know that Master P was coming to town. We told the kids that we had a surprise guest speaker for them that day. He waited in the back while the students arrived.

I introduced the guest speaker as someone who had come from the New Orleans projects and was now very successful. Master P came out singing one of his hit songs. He rocked that gym and brought down the house. Everyone was screaming and hollering. After his performance, he talked to the kids about the importance of education and staying in school. He took pictures with many of the kids and had poignant and personal conversations with a few of them afterward. Even the kids who usually cursed me every day on campus came running to hug me and thank me for bringing

Master P. to perform. I scored major points with them that day. They knew I cared enough to call in the heavy hitters.

After Master P spoke with them, I got on stage. My mother had come that day, and I wanted to introduce all of the students to her. My mom took the microphone and began to tell the students that I was in and out of jail as a kid. She shared with them how much my fate troubled her heart. She expressed how their actions could affect their parents, especially their mothers.

I began to think about all of the pain I'd caused in the past. All at once, I grabbed my mother around her shoulders, looked into her eyes, and then took the microphone. In front of hundreds of children, I told her how sorry I was for what I had done. I vowed to her, in front of that entire student body, that I would never repeat those mistakes again.

I could see the kid who'd hit me in the head several months earlier. He sat close to the stage and stared directly at me until he put his head in his hands. I imagined how lost he might have felt. How could he have any respect for his mother when she had no respect for herself or her children? Here I was, with my mother on stage, a classy lady who had put her love for me on full display, but his mother was probably at home, drugged up and beyond reproach. He began showing me the same respect I'd shown him. Respect was earned, and students knew when they were being disregarded and when they were being inspired. Later that week, he even gave me some information regarding a shooting that had occurred but was still under investigation.

I have been blessed to learn how to motivate kids. I came to know a man named Dr. Peter Scharf through a mutual connection with Khalil. Dr. Scharf was a renowned criminologist at Tulane University. While serving time in prison, Khalil had read about Peter and his teachings. When Khalil got to New Orleans and met up with Peter, they connected through their mutual affinity for helping kids get off the street.

Peter took a liking to me. He also had a big heart for helping at-risk youth. He taught me about Lawrence Kohlberg, a Jewish-American psychologist who specialized in research on moral education and reasoning. We shared the same passion and often got together to talk about youth-based strategies. He shared information with me on how to help these kids transform their trauma. We were particularly interested in evidence-based practices that were proven effective.

After he found out about my life and what I had gone through, he embraced me like a son. Every influential person in New Orleans, from the Mayor to the Chief of Police, Peter introduced me to all of them. Suddenly, I knew people in positions of power throughout the city on a first-name basis. I knew the judges and even had a connection with the head federal prosecutor.

Peter took off from work many times in order to visit the students in my classes. He'd ask them ethical questions like, "Would you steal medicine if your mother was sick?" Or, "Is it okay to sell drugs if there's no food in the house?" I often brought him back to the projects to talk to kids or chat about solutions with some older folks. He loved it. He'd call his wife and tell her, "Ameer has me in the projects all day again."

Peter was a funny, well-educated man who never cared much about how he dressed. News stations around the city called upon him to give his viewpoint on the crimes that were all too commonplace. He'd interview with an old t-shirt and jacket on. I came to love him more and more because he never disassociated himself from the poor.

He had no prejudice, and he was a humanist. He saw every person as a valued human being and felt that people acted the way they did because of the trauma they'd experienced during their upbringing. He also knew there was a great disparity in access to educational programs between black and white communities.

Peter tried several times to get me to commit to going to Tulane to further my education. He wanted to give me a free four-year scholarship, but my desire was not to become a psychologist, lawyer, or doctor. I knew I could have a greater impact with more kids on a larger scale by pursuing my passion for acting.

I was given the opportunity to lecture during Peter's classes at Tulane. As I walked around the campus, I used to think that if I were a younger man, this would have been the place I would've wanted to be. I made a point to hang out with all of the brightest minds, the young people who wanted to be the best in their class. At times, while I walked the campus halls, my emotions would sway toward negative thoughts about my place in life. I had missed this opportunity as a teenager. However, I was in control of my thoughts, and therefore, I would never allow what hadn't happened then to overshadow all that was possible now. I would dance with depression, but I tried with all my might not to allow the past to overtake me.

After my lectures, many students wrote papers about me. Whenever students wrote about how the lecture had influenced them, my spirits were always lifted. Though I hadn't attended college like any of these students, I was honored to be able to leave such an impression on their young minds.

Chapter 27

REFLECTIONS

I had sold dope. For all my best efforts not to, I had abused women—both physically and mentally. I had lied to get out of trouble. I had cheated to get ahead. I had murdered a fellow human being, and I had experienced many years locked away in prison. Although I have learned to take responsibility for who I am and what I've done, for a long time, I blamed my troubles solely on my dad and his absence from my early childhood. I still think growing up without a positive father figure really impacted how I developed.

I lived a life of crime for many years, and I believe that many of our problems in the black community stem from self-imposed limitations. In my mind, the impact of a fatherless childhood was the primary driver that allowed me to be lured into a violent and negative lifestyle. A good dad could have prevented me from turning to the streets and from the confusion of trying to identify with a male in my life worth emulating. There were none, so I had to make up my character as I went along. Add my learning difference and dyslexia to the equation, and it's no surprise I began to identify with the dark instead of the light. When the shame of not having a dad to identify with collides with the shame of not being able to read, the cards aren't just stacked, the ante is too high for a young boy to play. The streets taught me a game I could never win. I lost my sense of self before I had one. The dope game could only lead in one direction—a fast track to incarceration.

Countless men are sitting in prison who left their children behind without considering how it could, and would, affect them. With Kim's children, I felt firsthand how powerful being a father figure for your children could be and what a significant effect I had on their lives. My older brother Dash is an excellent example of a supportive father figure. He's always encouraged his children and showed up for his kids in positive ways. As a consequence of his guidance, they grew up educated and respectful, and all of them graduated from college.

As important as it is to grow into being a father, it's way too easy to become one. If men retained more responsibility to the women in their lives, there wouldn't be so many single mothers trying their best to raise kids on their own. A part-time dad cannot just jump right into the role after being absent for years. True fatherhood takes time, love, trust, and support. Eventually, kids see through deceit and selfish narcissism. To be respected as a 'real' father, not only does a man need to stick around, he has to work on himself and do better than his own parents did in raising the next generation.

When my own dad came back into my life after being absent for so many years, I fully accepted him, although my siblings were more skeptical. My dad had this destructive way of trying to make up for the lost time by trying to step in and correct or direct us as young adults. This tactic did not go over well with Dash and Russhan. I recall him telling Dash what he should do in a situation involving his kids. Dash went off on him, "Don't tell me what to do with my own kids. You don't know how to be a dad or raise kids." I could tell my dad was pissed, but we were grown men, and there was not much he could do. My dad had missed the sacred window of opportunity to gain Dash's respect growing up. My sister and brother never showed any respect for him. They never called him 'Daddy.' He hadn't earned our affection.

By the time our father came back into the picture, Dash and Russhan both had kids of their own. They knew how strong a parent's love could be, and they could not understand what circumstance could drive a parent to abandon their children. How could our dad have walked away from the three of us, we often wondered? My sister and brother still talk about his failures and how his lack of dedication affected them. The psychological effects of not having a father figure in her life and my sister's childhood sexual abuse contributed to her making poor choices with the men she chose to date. In part, relationships were pretty hard for her to negotiate because our dad wasn't there to be a good example of a version of maleness she would later be attracted to. Our absentee father's impact on his daughter's future relationships was painfully evident to her and us. Our dad's obligation to nurture and mentor his daughter hadn't been his priority, and he'd failed her miserably.

Why do so many black and white men leave their kids behind? If men had babies instead of women, I suspect the tendencies might be different. A male caregiver, a father who changes diapers and puts his kids first, this is the version of maleness I want to see in the black community. If only responsible dads were the rule and not the exception. The question of who raises children often troubles me when I think back to the kids in the projects and how much they need full parental support. I may not be an expert on the subject, but I can speak from experience.

Sexual education must happen earlier so teenagers and young adults can wait to become parents until they're old enough to know how much energy and dedication it takes to raise well-adjusted children. We need to teach our youth earlier about the realities of parenthood to understand how many resources are required to be present and wholly available to meet their children's needs.

Undereducated Black men in New Orleans are responsible for at least ninety percent of the murders committed in the projects. Most of the killers grew up in fatherless, single-parent households without much supervision. The black community has the highest incarceration rate, most single-parent families, and the highest school drop-out rates in the country. My neighbors growing up were amongst the largest percentage living below the poverty line.

Although systemic racism and educational inequity can't be blamed on irresponsible dads per se, these social issues are only made worse by a culture of patriarchy where the mistreatment of women is commonplace. Abandoning a mother to raise kids by herself is criminal. We can have no intergenerational healing without acknowledging the vicious cycle incarceration plays in destroying familial balance. The prison pipeline that separates families is a fate I barely escaped. Thankfully, I had no children to abandon while I was in prison.

Based on my experience, an absentee father is a symptom of much larger societal issues. All of the statistics I mentioned are highly interconnected. And having a strong father figure can give children a solid chance at overcoming some of the challenges they'll face. Substance abuse and drug and alcohol use also play a huge part in why dads abandon their families. Addiction is linked to poverty and poverty to addiction. When I got sober, I had the will to change and improve my lot in life. Before prison, my drug habit fueled my violence, and the violence was often a result of trafficking drugs. To be able to see the cause and effect from the inside out compelled me to write about my story.

Only through our shared experiences can we hope to sail through so many obstacles and reach a reimagined shore. All of these layered societal and familial issues would be eased if men were held to account and took the initiative to come back home and take responsibility for their families. A two-parent household allows both parents to face the rigors of parenthood with greater success. Dual-parent households give children the best chance to be provided for, feel protected, and be nurtured by their families. Thank God for the mothers and grandmothers who do their best to raise us. When we start to recall and honor the liberties our ancestors died for, then and only then can we begin to appreciate all that this country has to offer us.

Education is the key to escaping poverty. The education system becomes a safety net for kids who are forced to raise themselves. If that's the case, funding for effective intervention programs isn't optional but essential to societal repair. We must make sure that state funding is adequate enough to equalize public education so everyone, no matter what zip code or state they live in, can access the same educational resources.

In my twenties, getting my GED was a gateway to a better future. We can educate our teachers to recognize learning differences as early as possible. We can teach children the stories of the people who took the initiative and responsibility to carve our history in their image. Imagine an education system that leaves no child behind, for real. What if educational equity became a given and fairly empowered each child with the stories of heroes to aspire to. We can shape the change-makers of tomorrow by reshaping our schools today. When every man in prison is tested for dyslexia, when every student knows they're safe to learn, when the legislators pass more guidance on how to help teachers be successful in teaching literacy, no one will have to be a slave to the streets. We can choose family and a life in service to the kids who need our help the most.

My mother was still a teenager when she had my siblings and me. Her potential as an independent person, a woman, and an individual disappeared when she became a mother. Before she knew herself, she had to learn to mother. Although I have a lot of animosity toward my dad, I also have come to terms with the ways I've blamed my mother for my childhood. At a certain point in my adult life, I made the conscious choice to forgive her. I have never questioned her love for us, only her ability to raise us in a way where we didn't accumulate so many adverse childhood experiences (ACEs).

My hopes and dreams for the future are that we can wake up–as a culture and in our communities. I wish for each child, each citizen, to seize every opportunity this land has to offer and learn to have a broader vision for improved lives. Black people built America. We are some of the hardest working people in the world. There's nothing wrong with using assistance to get a step up and begin to build a better life, but when we become dependent on the system without trying to move forward, that mentality becomes a bigger problem.

If we don't make time for our kids right now, then they will end up doing time later. If we don't read books to our kids, we will end up posting money for their bail after they get booked. If our love and affection are too costly to give now, they may end up doing life behind bars. Prison is that serious. Time and freedom are the most expensive things to lose. I wish someone would have really shown me when I was younger how to protect my future from the misery of being trapped in a cycle of violence.

Most of the people I grew up with or spoke about in this book are either dead or in prison. In the end, their choices were often catastrophic–what they chose to do, they could not undo.

Doe Doe got into the rap music business, bought a Range Rover, and was living it up. Everyone knew Doe Doe was a contract killer. He was feared in the streets. One day, in the ninth ward in the projects, he was gunned down. The killer dropped six shots into Doe Doe's chest and one to his head.

Mike eventually lost everything he'd worked for. I had looked up to him when I was younger. At age sixty-five, he was working at a car dealership washing cars.

Bernie ended up having a stroke and will remain in hospice care for the rest of his life. He doesn't even know who he is.

Don was in Los Angeles and sentenced to ten years in federal prison. Now he is out and working at a car wash on La Brea.

At one time, each of these men had big money to spend, but now they live below the poverty line.

How could my life have turned out differently if I had made better choices earlier? Sometimes the path of least resistance, or the 'easy' route, is anything but easy. Choosing any other path was too difficult for me. My undiagnosed disability convinced me I had fewer options. I knew there were other ways to live life. I saw other kids headed in better directions. But my influences were unavoidable, and the trifecta of education failure, drugs, and poverty was too much for my young brain to resist the enticements of street life.

There are kids out there who have never yet experienced prison. There are kids who are waiting to be pulled back from the brink of making a life-altering decision they cannot take back. I never felt like I had the potential or ability to choose any other path. I was swept up in the drug life, and the undercurrent overwhelmed me and took me under. No life jacket, no buoy could have kept me afloat. Looking back, I regret so many of those choices.

One day, when I was sitting on set, Blair Underwood told me I should write a book about my life experiences. I decided to take his advice. Writing about my life has helped me quit ruminating and looking backward for a suitable or tidy explanation and focus on the future. The 'why' things happened the way they did isn't as important as the 'how' I can help spare today's young people the same fate. Through my *Dyslexia Awareness Foundation* and *Good Works Project*, I've discovered hope can help heal all of us.

Education is the key to breaking the chains that bind us. To free ourselves from any past limitations or versions of how we may have grown up, and realize who we are capable of becoming, now that's a message worth the effort of educational reform. Redemption is contagious, and that's what I hope to spread. The inspiration to have a complete metamorphosis into a better version of oneself needs wings.

The more good people we have to serve as examples of how to become something good out in the world, the better. People *can* change. Children are worth our collective time and attention. I say to them, "Don't let anything stop you from carving a new way home."

Let's take a few other people along with us when we move forward. The fruition of our labor results in our children's health and well-being and all the others who may follow our lead. Every human being deserves to read and learn to communicate without violence. I am a living testament to the power and possibility of second chances and the unlocked potential education provides.

ABOUT AMEER BARAKA

Ameer Baraka is an award-winning and Daytime Emmy Nominated Actor, author, dyslexia advocate, youth mentor, and prison coach.

Born to humble beginnings in New Orleans, Louisiana, Ameer had an early life that was as gloomy and ill-fated as a young life could be. In and out of the prison system as a kid for transgressions ranging from youthful indiscretions to major crimes, he was seemingly on a one-way trip to oblivion. Almost illiterate when he went to prison, he was diagnosed with dyslexia and learned to read in his mid-twenties while behind bars.

Recognizing how education and ability to read have changed his life, Ameer is dedicated to inspiring young people with his message that they, too, can overcome meager beginnings and obstacles on their way to eventually triumph through hard work, dedication, the pursuit of education, and strong faith.

Ameer is dedicated to working with at-risk youth in their own crime-infested public housing projects to get them off the streets and into the classroom while exposing them to better life opportunities. He mentors incarcerated youth to inspire and prepare them to learn life and career skills and make better future life decisions. His work also includes providing racial bias training to police departments to identify and mitigate implicit and unconscious biases and prejudices based on a person's racial identity.

Proud of every aspect of his life, including his brief stint in the Louisiana State Penitentiary, he now travels the world, speaking at colleges, universities, corporations, and youth organizations. He uses all his life experiences to increase dyslexia awareness.

RESOURCES

Learning Ally <learningally.org>

Decoding Dyslexia <decodingdyslexia.net>

International Dyslexia Association <dyslexiaida.org>

The Yale Center for Dyslexia & Creativity <dyslexia.yale.edu>

National Center for Learning Disabilities <ncld.org>

Understood <understood.org>

Orton-Gillingham Academy <ortonacademy.org>

The Neuro-development of Words – NOW! <nowprograms.com>

Made in United States
Troutdale, OR
01/21/2025